Merlin magically caused a marble block, four feet long on each edge, to appear in the square in front of St. Paul's cathedral in London.

He placed an anvil of solid iron on top of the block and thrust a sword into the anvil to a depth of half its blade. This sword was the most wonderful that anyone had ever seen. Its blade was of glistening blue steel, its hilt of beautifully fashioned gold set with many gems. The sword shone with wonderful brightness in the sunlight. These words appeared in gold letters on the marble block: "Whoever pulls this sword from the anvil is the rightful king of Britain."

A Background Note about
King Arthur and His Nights

The tales recounted in *King Arthur and His Knights* have their origins in Celtic myth and legend. Did King Arthur ever exist? Scholars believe that the character might have been inspired, in part, by a Celtic warlord who lived around 500 A.D. and halted the advance of Saxons into western Britain.

However, the society depicted in the book most resembles that of Christian medieval Europe. In essence, knights were mounted soldiers and police who served a particular lord to whom they pledged loyalty. Squires, who were training to become knights, served particular knights. With rare exception lords, knights, and squires were of noble birth.

HOWARD PYLE

KING ARTHUR

and His

KNIGHTS

Edited, and with an Afterword,
by Joan Dunayer

TP THE TOWNSEND LIBRARY

KING ARTHUR AND
HIS KNIGHTS

TP THE TOWNSEND LIBRARY

For more titles in the Townsend Library,
visit our website: **www.townsendpress.com**

All new material in this edition is
copyright © 2007 by Townsend Press.
Printed in the United States of America

0 9 8 7 6 5 4 3 2

ISBN 13: 978-1-59194-074-6
ISBN 10: 1-59194-074-5

Library of Congress Control Number:
2006935723

Contents

Afterword

Chapter 1

In ancient days there lived a king named Uther Pendragon. Two men greatly assisted King Uther in all that he did. One was the powerful wizard Merlin, who gave Uther political advice. The other was the famous warrior Sir Ulfius, who gave Uther aid and advice in battle. With the help of Merlin and Ulfius, Uther overcame all of his enemies and became king of Britain.

After Uther had ruled Britain for some years, he married a gentle, beautiful lady named Igraine. This noble lady was the widow of Gorlois, Duke of Tintegal. Igraine had two daughters from her marriage to Gorlois: Morgause and Morgan le Fay, a famous sorceress. After marrying Uther, Igraine brought her daughters with her to his court. Morgause married King Urien of Gore, and Morgan married King Lot of Orkney and the Isles.

Uther and Igraine had a son. He was beautiful, large, and strong. While the baby was still in his cradle of gold and ultramarine, Merlin said to

Uther, "Lord, I foresee that you soon will fall sick with a fever and die. This baby will be in great danger; many enemies will want to hold him captive or kill him so that he can't become king. I beg you to permit Sir Ulfius and me to take the baby to some safe place where he can be hidden until he grows to manhood and is able to protect himself."

Uther replied, "Merlin, when my time comes to die, I believe I'll accept my end with good grace. However, if your prophecy about my son is true, the danger is great and he should be taken to a safe place. My son is the most precious thing that I'll leave to my people."

Merlin and Ulfius took the baby away at night to a secret place. Shortly after, Uther died of a fever, as Merlin had foretold. Britain fell into disorder. Every lesser king contended against every other to be king of Britain. Wicked knights and barons attacked travelers on the roads, holding them for ransom if they were wealthy and killing them if they weren't. It was common to see dead people lying by the roadside.

Nearly eighteen years passed in great affliction. Then the Archbishop of Canterbury summoned Merlin and said, "Merlin, people say that you're the world's wisest man. Can you find some way to heal this ailing realm? Choose a king who will be a good ruler, so that we can be happy again, as we were when Uther Pendragon ruled Britain."

Merlin said, "My lord, Britain soon will have a king who will be wiser, greater, and more praiseworthy even than Uther Pendragon. He'll replace disorder and war with order and peace. This king will be of Uther Pendragon's royal blood."

"Can you foretell when this king will come?" the archbishop asked. "How will we know him? Many unworthy men proclaim themselves to be the rightful king."

Merlin said, "If I have your permission to practice my magic, I'll arrange a challenge. If anyone can meet it, the world will know that he's the rightful king."

"You have my permission," the archbishop said.

Merlin magically caused a marble block, four feet long on each edge, to appear in the square in front of St. Paul's cathedral in London. He placed an anvil of solid iron on top of the block and thrust a sword into the anvil to a depth of half its blade. This sword was the most wonderful that anyone had ever seen. Its blade was of glistening blue steel, its hilt of beautifully fashioned gold set with many gems. The sword shone with wonderful brightness in the sunlight. These words appeared in gold letters on the marble block: "Whoever pulls this sword from the anvil is the rightful king of Britain."

When Merlin had accomplished this magic,

he asked the archbishop to summon the country's leading men to gather on Christmas day and, one by one, try to pull out the sword. The archbishop did as Merlin advised. The summons caused a great stir throughout the land. Everyone asked everyone else, "Who will pull out the sword? Who will be our king?" Most people thought it would be someone who already was a king.

As Christmas approached, the whole world seemed to head to London. The highways and byways became filled with travelers. Kings, lords, knights, ladies, squires, pages—all headed to see the attempts to pull the sword from the anvil. Every inn and castle was filled with travelers. Tents and pavilions were set up along the wayside to accommodate those who couldn't find shelter indoors.

When the archbishop saw the multitudes that were assembling, he said to Merlin, "It would be strange if no one among all these great kings and noble lords was worthy to be king."

Merlin smiled and said, "Don't be surprised, my lord, if none of those who appear so worthy turn out to be worthy. And don't be surprised if someone unknown proves worthy."

Chapter 2

The high-born knight Sir Ector of Bonmaison was among those who came to London. Called "the trustworthy knight," he never violated anyone's trust. Everyone who knew Ector greatly respected him. He owned seven castles, fertile lands with villages, and vast forests. Ector had two sons. The elder was Sir Kay, a young, brave knight already renowned for several actions as a soldier. The younger was eighteen-year-old Arthur, who was serving with good repute as Kay's squire.

When a messenger brought Ector word of the archbishop's mandate, Ector immediately summoned Kay and Arthur. They headed to London with many squires, pages, and servants. Upon arriving at the London field where many other knights and powerful lords were camping, Ector erected a green silk pavilion and a banner with his family's coat of arms, a black griffin on a green background. Each of the many pavilions on the field had a banner. There were so many fluttering banners of different colors that in places they nearly hid the sky. Twelve kings and seven dukes gathered, accompanied by lords, ladies, squires, and pages.

The archbishop had commanded that a jousting tournament be held in a field near St. Paul's cathedral three days before Christmas. Many knights of high birth, position, and reputation applied to participate. Three heralds made sure that all participants were of sufficiently noble lineage.

When Kay learned of the tournament, he said to Ector, "Father, I wish to participate in the tournament. I'm of sufficiently high birth and wealth. I want to show those who have gathered that I'm worthy of knighthood. My participation will honor you and our house. Do I have your permission to participate?"

"Yes, my son. I hope that God will give you strength and such grace of spirit that you'll do credit to yourself and your family."

Kay went to the heralds and submitted his qualifications. To his joy the heralds entered his name as a knight contestant. Kay chose Arthur as his squire. Arthur would accompany Kay onto the field of battle, carrying Kay's spear and pennant. Arthur was overjoyed at the honor bestowed on Kay and him.

The day of the tournament at least twenty

thousand lords and ladies assembled to watch the contest. Nobles filled so many seats and benches and sat so close together that they seemed to form a solid wall around the field of battle. With so many ladies and lords watching, the contestants were eager to triumph.

The archbishop's stall and throne were erected in the center of the nobles. Above the throne was a purple canopy emblazoned with silver lilies. The throne was draped with purple velvet embroidered, alternately, with the figure of St. George in gold and with silver crosses encircled by gold halos.

When everything was ready, a herald stepped in front of the archbishop's throne and blew a trumpet. The contestants took their assigned places—ninety-three of them at the field's north end and ninety-six of them at its south end. The field glittered with sunlight on polished armor. Kay was at the north end. Although the knights at that end numbered three fewer than those at the south end, they composed the stronger group because some of them had exceptional strength.

All of the knights prepared their spears and shields. The herald blew his trumpet, paused, and blew it again. At the second blast the two opposing teams of knights rushed toward each other with such fury that the earth shook beneath the horses' feet. The two sides met in the middle of the field. The clamor of breaking spears was so terrible that those who heard it were appalled. The air was filled with flying splinters of wood. Some ladies screamed.

In that first clash seventy knights were thrown, many of them trampled beneath the horses' hooves. When the two sides withdrew to their stations, the ground was covered with spear and armor fragments. Many knights lay amid the wreckage. Some of them tried to rise but couldn't; others lay as still as death. Squires and pages ran to the fallen men and bore them to places of safety. Servants ran and gathered up the weapon fragments. The field soon was cleared.

No knight had done better than Kay. He had successfully resisted the assault of two opponents who had simultaneously directed their spears at him. Kay had struck one assailant so hard that he had fallen backwards off his horse, rolled over in the dust three times, and landed several feet away. Seeing what Kay had done, his nearby team members had cheered him. Kay was greatly pleased.

Back at his station, each knight gave his spear to his squire. The next assault would be with swords. When the herald again blew his trumpet, each knight drew his sword with such readiness that a great splendor of blades flashed in the air. The herald trumpeted a second time, and each knight rushed forward. The knights delivered vehement blows.

Kay knocked down five knights, one after the

other. Several knights of the opposing team tried to hit him. Sir Balamorgineas was among them. He was so large that he rode head and shoulders above any other knight and so strong that he usually could withstand the assault of three knights at once. He cried out to Kay, "Ho! Knight of the black griffin, turn this way and do battle with *me!*"

Kay cheerfully turned toward Balamorgineas. Full of youthful fire, he wasn't afraid to fight anyone. "I'll do battle with you!" Kay cried. "I'll hurl you down as I did the others." With all his might Kay struck Balamorgineas on his helmet. Balamorgineas never had received such a stunning blow. He grabbed the horn of his saddle to keep from falling. Kay's blow was so fierce that his sword blade snapped off at the hilt and flew high into the air, leaving him weaponless. Balamorgineas recovered and saw that Kay was at his mercy. Enraged by the blow he had received, he prepared to strike Kay. Three of Kay's teammates quickly thrust in between Balamorgineas and Kay, allowing Kay to escape, unharmed, to the barriers.

Arthur ran to Kay with a goblet of spiced wine. Kay lifted the front of his helmet to drink. His face was covered with blood and sweat. When he had drunk, he said to Arthur, "I've broken my sword. Fetch me another. I'm going to win our house much glory today."

"Where can I get you a sword?" Arthur said.

"Go to Father's pavilion."

Arthur leaped over the barrier and raced to Ector's pavilion in the meadows. But he couldn't find a suitable sword there. Desperate, he remembered the sword in the anvil in front of St. Paul's. "That sword would do very well," he thought. So Arthur ran to the cathedral. No one was around; everyone was at the tournament. Arthur leaped onto the marble block, grasped the sword's hilt, and easily pulled the sword out. He wrapped the sword in his cloak so that no one would see it shining, leaped down from the marble block, and hurried with the sword to the battlefield.

Kay was waiting impatiently. "Do you have a sword?"

"Yes," Arthur said. He opened his cloak and showed Kay the sword.

Immediately recognizing the sword, Kay was dumbfounded. "Where did you get that sword?"

"I couldn't find any sword in Father's pavilion, so I took this one from the marble block in front of St. Paul's. It came out easily."

Kay pondered the situation. "Arthur is hardly more than a child," he thought. "He doesn't know the significance of what he's done. Why shouldn't I say that I'm the one who pulled the sword out of the anvil?" Kay then said, "Give me the sword and cloak. Don't tell anyone about this. Ask Father to go to our pavilion right away."

Chapter 3

Arthur hurried to Ector, who sat amid members of his household, and said, "Father, Kay asks that you come to the pavilion right away. He has a very strange expression. I think something extraordinary has happened." Ector wondered what could be so important that Kay would ask him to come at that time. He and Arthur went to the pavilion. Kay was already there, his face white and his eyes glittering.

"My son, what's the matter?" Ector asked. Kay took his father by the hand and brought him to a table that stood inside the pavilion. The cloak was on the table. Kay opened it. There lay the sword from the anvil, its hilt and blade glistening. Ector cried, "Isn't this the sword that was embedded in the anvil in front of St. Paul's?"

"Yes," Kay said.

"How did you get it?"

Kay hesitated. "I broke my sword in the tournament and found this sword to replace it."

"What do you mean by 'found'?" Ector said.

"Did you draw this sword from the anvil? If so, you're the rightful king of Britain! In that case you'll be able to thrust the sword back into the anvil."

Kay was troubled. "Who can thrust a sword into solid iron?"

"That feat is no greater than pulling it out," Ector replied. "If you pulled it out, you can push it back in."

Kay didn't say anything. He thought, "If Arthur easily pulled the sword out, why shouldn't I be able to put it back in? Surely I'm as worthy as he is." Kay wrapped the sword in the cloak again. He, Ector, and Arthur went to the anvil. Kay mounted the marble block and looked at the anvil. It was completely smooth, without so much as a scratch. Feeling that the task was impossible, Kay nevertheless tried to thrust the sword into the anvil. He set the point of the sword to the iron and bore down on it with all his strength. He couldn't even dent the iron. He gave up, saying to his father, "No one can perform such a feat."

"Then, how did you manage to draw the sword out?" Ector said.

Arthur said, "Father, may I speak?"

"Yes, my son."

"I'm the one who drew the sword from the anvil."

Ector was amazed. "Try to put the sword into the anvil," he said to Arthur.

Arthur took the sword from Kay, leaped onto the marble block, set the point of the sword on the anvil, and bore down on the sword. It smoothly penetrated to the anvil's center and stood fast, half buried. Arthur then quickly took the sword out again and thrust it back in. Ector cried, "What miracle is this?"

When Arthur came down from the marble block, Ector kneeled before him and set his hands together palm to palm as if in prayer. Pained, Arthur cried, "Father, why are you kneeling to me?"

Ector replied, "I'm not your father. Clearly,

the blood of kings flows in your veins. Otherwise you couldn't have handled the sword as you did."

Kay thought, "Is Arthur really a king?"

Weeping, Arthur said, "Father, what are you saying? Please don't kneel to me!"

Ector rose. "Arthur, the time has come for you to know the truth. Eighteen years ago the wise wizard and prophet Merlin came to me. He showed me King Uther's signet ring and commanded me by virtue of that ring to meet him at midnight at the royal castle's back gate. Merlin ordered me to maintain absolute secrecy. As instructed, I met Merlin at midnight. King Uther's chief knight, Sir Ulfius, also was there. Merlin had in his arms something wrapped in a fine scarlet cloak. He opened the folds of the cloak, and, in the light of Sir Ulfius' lantern, I saw a fair, strong infant wrapped in swaddling clothes. The infant was you. Merlin commanded me to take you, call you Arthur, rear you as my own child, and tell no one that you weren't really my son. I did as Merlin instructed. I myself never knew your father's identity. Now I suspect that you're the son of King Uther himself."

"Oh!" Arthur lamented. "I've lost my father. I'd rather have a father than be a king."

Arthur, Kay, and Ector now saw two tall, noble-looking men approaching. They recognized Merlin and Ulfius. After an exchange of greetings, Ector said, "Merlin, here's the boy you brought me eighteen years ago. Look how he's grown into manhood."

"I know him well," Merlin said. "I've kept watch over him all this time. Britain's hopes lie with him. Today I looked into my magic mirror and saw him pull the sword from the anvil. Arthur, I foresee your being Britain's greatest king. Sir Ector, guard him well for three more days."

Ector said to Arthur, "I have a request."

"You can have anything in the world that's mine to give," Arthur said.

"I beg you to make Kay your seneschal when you're king."

"I'll do that and more," Arthur said. "You'll always be my father." Taking Ector's head in his hands, Arthur kissed Ector on his forehead and cheeks.

Kay stood silent and motionless. He didn't know whether to rejoice or to resent that Arthur had been exalted above him.

Chapter 4

On Christmas morning, thousands of people of all ranks gathered in front of St. Paul's to watch the contest to pull out the sword. A canopy of many-colored embroidered cloth had been set up over the sword and anvil, and a platform had been built around the marble block. Nearby was a throne for the archbishop, who would oversee the competition.

Mid-morning the archbishop came with great pomp and took his seat on the throne. His court of clerks and knights gathered around him. Nineteen kings and sixteen dukes had come to compete—each of high estate and each hoping to prove that he was Britain's rightful king. Several of these nobles now demanded to be tested. At the archbishop's command, a herald sounded a trumpet, signaling the start of the competition.

King Lot, who had eleven knights and five squires with him, immediately stepped forward and mounted the platform. He saluted the archbishop and then put his hands to the sword. Lot bent his body and pulled on the sword with great strength, but he couldn't move the blade. He tried four more times without success. Angry and indignant, he stepped down.

Lot's brother-in-law, King Urien, was next. He, too, failed. Then came King Fion of Scotland, King Mark of Cornwall, and all the other kings and dukes who had come to compete. All failed. People said to one another, "If these great kings and dukes have failed, who can succeed? The task is impossible."

Six of the worthiest kings then asked the archbishop to choose a king of Britain from among the kings who were gathered. They agreed to abide by his decision. The archbishop was troubled. "Merlin is honest and wise, and he told me to hold this competition," he thought. "The right person must not have tried yet." The archbishop said to the kings, "My lords, be patient somewhat longer. If no one succeeds within the next quarter hour, I'll do as you ask and select a king from among you."

Merlin, Ulfius, Ector, Kay, and Arthur now approached the platform. Murmuring in wonder, the crowd made way for them. Arthur wore orange clothes embroidered with silver threads. People commented, "That youth is very handsome. Who is he?"

Merlin brought Arthur to the archbishop and said, "Lord, this youth has come to compete."

"By what right does he compete?" the archbishop asked.

"By the best right in the world," Merlin answered. "He's the son of King Uther and Queen Igraine."

The archbishop cried out in amazement, as did spectators who stood close enough to hear Merlin's words. "Is this true, Merlin?" the archbishop said. "Until now no one has heard of King Uther's having had a son."

"Only a few have known," Merlin replied. He explained why Arthur's birthright had been kept secret. "Sir Ulfius will attest to the truth of what I say. So will Sir Ector of Bonmaison, who raised Arthur as his son." Ulfius and Ector confirmed the truth of Merlin's words.

"I don't doubt such honorable witnesses," the archbishop said. He looked at Arthur and smiled.

Arthur said, "Lord, do I have your permission to handle the sword?"

"Yes," the archbishop answered, "and may God's grace be with you."

Arthur went to the marble block, took hold of the sword's hilt, bent his body, and easily pulled out the sword. He swung the sword around his head three times. It flashed like lightning. Then he pushed it back into the anvil. The people cheered. While they shouted, Arthur again pulled out the sword and pushed it back in.

All of the kings and dukes were amazed. Some of them humbly acknowledged Arthur's triumph. Others withdrew and, standing apart, said, "Shall a beardless boy be set above us and made king of the entire realm? No." Others said, "Merlin and Sir Ulfius are exalting this unknown boy in order to elevate themselves." Arthur's brothers-in-law Lot and Urien were especially bitter.

When the archbishop saw the discontent of these kings and dukes, he said to them, "This youth has accomplished what none of you could. Accept him as your king." However, these lords left filled with anger. Other kings and dukes saluted and congratulated Arthur. King Leodegrance of Cameliard was among these friendly well-wishers. The multitude acknowledged Arthur and crowded around him shouting with joy.

All this while Ector and Kay stood to one side. They grieved that Arthur now seemed so far above them that they wouldn't be able to approach him anymore. After a while Arthur noticed that they looked downcast. He went to them, took first one and then the other by the hand, and kissed each on the cheek. Then Ector and Kay were glad again.

When Arthur left the cathedral square, a great crowd followed him, cheering him as king of Britain. Those nearest to him touched the hem of his garments. Arthur felt joy.

Although some kings continued to object to Arthur's becoming king, other kings, many barons and knights, and the general public considered Arthur the rightful ruler. The archbishop anointed and crowned Arthur at St. Paul's.

Those opposed to Arthur's kingship prepared to war against him. With Merlin's advice Arthur made friends and allies of other kings. Arthur and these allies fought two great wars with his enemies and won both. In the second war Arthur defeated his enemies so entirely that they couldn't hope to unite in war against him ever again.

To ensure peace with his brothers-in-law Lot and Urien, Arthur had Lot's sons Gawain and Gaheris, and Urien's son Ewaine, live at his court. Arthur drove his enemy King Pellinore into the forest and his enemy King Ryence into the mountains of North Wales. He subjugated other hostile kings to his will. So the land was at peace.

As he had promised, Arthur made Kay his seneschal. He made Ulfius his chamberlain, Merlin his counselor, and Sir Bodwin his constable. These men enhanced Arthur's glory and power. As Arthur's renown spread, many knights were attracted to his service.

Chapter 5

One warm spring day, Arthur and his court were traveling through the forest. They paused in the cool shade of trees. Arthur rested on a scarlet cloth spread over rushes. While he dozed, a number of his knights cheerfully conversed.

The gathering stirred at the approach of a wounded knight, held on his horse by a blond page. The page's clothes, the knight's clothes, and the horse's trappings all were white and sky blue. On the knight's shield was one silver lily on a sky-blue background. The knight's face was pale and drooped on his breast. His eyes were glazed. His clothes were blood-stained from a large wound in his side.

Arthur awoke and said, "What sad sight is this? Hurry, my lords. Aid this knight. Sir Kay, bring that young page here." A number of knights hurried to the wounded knight and conveyed him to Arthur's pavilion, which had been pitched nearby. Arthur's personal physician attended to the knight. Arthur asked the page,

"Who's your master? How was he wounded?"

"Lord, my master is Sir Miles of the White Fountain. Far north of here he's the lord of seven castles and several noble estates. Two weeks ago he and I set out because he wanted to seek adventure. He overcame six knights at various places and sent them all to his castle to tell his wife of his valor. This morning we came upon a beautiful castle surrounded by lawns and flower gardens. Three blond young women dressed in red satin tossed a golden ball to one another. As we approached, they stopped. The tallest asked Sir Miles where he was going. He answered that he was a knight seeking adventure. The three women laughed. The tallest one said, 'I can supply you with an adventure.' My master said, 'Fair lady, please tell me.' This lady then told Sir Miles to follow a particular path to a stone bridge that crossed a turbulent river. She said that there he'd find enough adventure to satisfy any man. So my master and I went there. Beyond the bridge was a castle with a tall tower. In front of the castle was a wide, level lawn of well-trimmed grass. Immediately beyond the bridge was an apple tree from which many shields hung. Halfway across the bridge was a single black shield. A brass hammer hung beside it. These words appeared in red beneath the shield: 'Whoever strikes this shield does so at his peril.' Sir Miles seized the hammer and struck the shield with such force that it rang like thunder. The castle's gate dropped, and a knight emerged. He was dressed from head to foot in black armor. His clothes and his horse's trappings also were entirely black. When the Black Knight saw my master, he swiftly rode across the meadow to the other end of the bridge, where he drew rein. He saluted my master and yelled, 'Sir Knight, why did you strike that shield? Because of your boldness, I'm going to take your shield and hang it on that tree with all the others.' My master replied, 'To do that, you'll have to overcome me.' Then they prepared to joust. They raced toward each other, meeting in the middle of the bridge with great force. My master's spear burst into splinters, but the Black Knight's remained intact. It pierced Sir Miles' shield and penetrated his side. Sir Miles and his horse were thrown. My master was too gravely wounded to get up. The Black Knight took my master's shield and added it to the shields hanging from the apple tree. Without paying any more attention to Sir Miles, he rode back into his castle. The gate closed behind him. With great difficulty I got Sir Miles onto his horse and started out in search of help."

"I deeply regret that a stranger was treated so discourteously within my kingdom and so near my court," Arthur said. "It certainly was discourteous to leave a fallen knight on the ground without even asking how badly he was hurt, and even more discourteous to take away the shield of a knight who had done good battle."

All the knights of the king's court agreed. Griflet, a favorite squire of the king, kneeled before Arthur and said, "My king, please make me a knight. Let me find this unkind knight, overcome him, and take back the shields that he has hung on the apple tree."

Arthur was troubled because Griflet had no combat experience. "You're too young to deal with such a powerful knight," he said.

"I beg you," Griflet pleaded.

"Very well," Arthur said, "but I fear that you'll be hurt."

That night Griflet prayed in a forest chapel. In the morning he received the Sacrament. Then Arthur made him a knight, fastening gold spurs onto Griflet's heels with his own hands. Griflet mounted his horse and rode off singing with joy.

Sir Miles died of his wound. That afternoon Arthur sat waiting with great anxiety for word of Griflet. Toward evening some of his servants hurried to him to say that Griflet was returning but without his shield and apparently badly wounded. Soon after, Griflet appeared, held on his horse by two knights of Arthur's court. Griflet's head hung down on his breast. His new armor was broken and covered with blood and dust. Arthur's heart contracted with sorrow.

At Arthur's bidding, Griflet was laid on a couch in the royal pavilion. Arthur's physician found that the head of a spear and part of its shaft still pierced Griflet's side. "Oh!" Arthur cried. "My dear young knight, what happened?"

In a weak voice Griflet said, "I went through the forest until I came upon the three young women encountered by Sir Miles. They directed me to the apple tree hung with shields. I struck the Black Knight's shield, and he rode out to fight me. However, upon seeing me he said that he wouldn't fight anyone so young and inexperienced. He advised me to withdraw, but I refused. Then he attacked. My spear burst into pieces, and his pierced my side. He hung my shield with the others. Then he lifted me back onto my horse." Griflet was in great pain.

Angry and distressed, Arthur declared that he himself would confront the Black Knight. Arthur's knights tried to dissuade him, but he was determined. That evening Arthur was too upset to eat or sleep. He paced his pavilion, waiting for dawn. As soon as the birds began to chirp and the east to brighten, Arthur summoned his two squires. With their assistance he put on his armor. He mounted a white horse and departed.

About noon Arthur saw before him a wide and gently sloping valley filled with flowers and crossed by a silver stream. A handsome castle stood in the middle of the valley. It had tall red roofs and many bright windows. Arthur saw the three blond young women, dressed in red satin, playing ball on a lawn. As he approached, they stopped tossing the ball. The three women smiled at Arthur. They thought he was very handsome and gallant-looking. One of the women asked Arthur where he was going. He replied, "Fair lady, I'm looking for the Black Knight who has overcome so many other knights and taken their shields. I intend to challenge him. Please tell me where I can find him."

"Good heavens!" the woman cried. "Within two days two other knights have gone against the Black Knight. Both were severely wounded. That castle and this valley, called the Valley of Delight, belong to us. If you insist on fighting the Black Knight, at least let us give you food and drink first." She blew an ivory whistle that hung from a gold chain around her neck. In response three pages dressed in red came from the castle, carrying a silver table covered with a white cloth. Five more pages dressed in red followed, bearing dried fruits, sugar-coated nuts, loaves of white bread, and flagons of white wine. Hungry and thirsty, Arthur eagerly dismounted and seated himself at the table. He ate with relish and conversed with the women, who sat beside him and listened to him with great interest and cheerfulness. Arthur didn't reveal his identity.

Having satisfied his hunger and thirst, Arthur mounted his horse. Walking alongside as Arthur slowly rode, the women led him across the valley a little way. When they reached a path that led into a dark forest, one of the women said, "That's the way you must go. Farewell and good luck. You're the most pleasant knight who has come here in a long time."

Arthur saluted the ladies and rode away. He soon came to a place where charcoal burners plied their trade. Many mounds of earth were smoking with smoldering logs. The smell of the dampened fires filled the air. As Arthur approached, he saw in the clearing three sooty fellows holding long knives. They pursued a white-bearded old man richly dressed in black. While his horse stood nearby, the old man ran here and there, trying to escape.

Crying "Stop, villains!" Arthur spurred his horse and lowered his spear. He drove down on the men with a thunderous noise. When the three cutthroats saw an armed knight bearing down on them, they cried out in fear, dropped their knives, and fled into the forest. Arthur rode up to the old man. "Merlin!" he exclaimed in surprise. "I think those men would have killed you if I hadn't shown up."

"Lord, it only looked that way," Merlin replied. "I could easily have saved myself as soon as I wanted to. You face far greater danger. Take me with you. Otherwise you'll surely suffer great sorrow and pain."

"Thank you. I accept your offer."

gradually

Chapter 6

Arthur and Merlin rode through the forest, which gradually thinned. Ahead, a river rushed through a dark glen. A stone bridge crossed the river, beyond which was a smooth, level lawn. Beyond this lawn was a tall, forbidding castle that seemed to rise out of the rocks on which it was built. Halfway across the bridge were a black shield and brass hammer. On the far side of the river was an apple tree whose branches were hung with many shields. Some of these shields were clean and unbroken; others were dirty, blood-stained, and broken.

"There must be a hundred shields hanging on that tree!" Arthur exclaimed. "Any knight who can defeat so many others must be amazingly strong and brave."

Merlin replied, "My lord, you can consider yourself lucky if your shield doesn't also hang there by the end of the day."

"As God wills," Arthur said steadfastly. "My desire to fight the Black Knight is even stronger than before. Think what honor I'd gain if I over-came him!" Arthur urged his horse forward. On the bridge he read the challenge written in red letters beneath the shield: "Whoever strikes this shield does so at his peril." Arthur seized the hammer and struck the shield so violently that the sound echoed back from the castle's walls.

The castle's gate dropped, and a huge knight whose armor, clothes, and trappings all were black approached. The Black Knight's horse crossed the smooth grass with a stately gait. Reaching the bridgehead, the Black Knight drew rein and called out, "Sir Knight, why did you strike my shield? For your discourtesy I'll take your shield and hang it on that apple tree, where many others already hang. Give me your shield, or prepare to joust. If you joust with me, you'll surely suffer great injury and pain."

"Thank you for allowing me a choice," Arthur said, "but God, not you, will decide whether or not you take my shield. Unkind knight, I've come here expressly to joust with you and try to take back all the shields that hang in that tree. Prepare yourself."

The Black Knight turned his horse's head, rode back some distance across the lawn, and took a stand. Arthur, too, took up a position on the lawn. Each knight prepared his spear and shield, then shouted and spurred his horse. The horses rushed forward. Arthur and the Black

Knight met in the middle of the field, crashing together like thunderbolts. Their spears burst into splinters. Their horses staggered back but remained on their feet.

Arthur, who was considered Britain's strongest knight, was amazed that his powerful blow hadn't thrown his opponent. "Sir Knight, I don't know who you are," he said, "but you're the strongest knight I've ever met. Please dismount so that we can continue our battle on foot, using swords."

"No," the Black Knight said. "I won't stop jousting until one of us is thrown." He then shouted, "Ho!" The castle's gate opened, and two tall squires dressed in black with crimson patches ran out, each holding a large ash spear. Arthur chose one of the spears; the Black Knight took the other. Each returned to his station.

Once again Arthur and the Black Knight charged each other on horseback. Once again they struck each other so forcefully that their spears shattered. As before, Arthur proposed that they fight on foot, but the Black Knight said no. The two again received new spears and charged each other. Arthur's spear shattered as it struck the Black Knight's shield. But the Black Knight's spear didn't break, even though it pierced through the center of Arthur's shield. The blow was so powerful that the straps of Arthur's saddle burst. He and his horse were thrown backward.

Arthur jumped from his saddle with such skill that he landed on his feet, but his horse was thrown. At first Arthur was dizzy. When he recovered, he felt great anger. The Black Knight sat nearby on his horse. Arthur ran to him and, catching his horse's bridle rein, roared, "Come down, Black Knight! Fight me on foot with your sword!"

"No," the Black Knight said. "I threw you, so give me your shield and go your way."

"I won't!" Arthur cried. "I won't leave until one of us has completely conquered the other!" Still holding the rein of the Black Knight's horse, Arthur yanked the horse backward. The Black Knight was forced to jump from his saddle to avoid falling to the ground. He was furious.

The Black Knight and Arthur drew their swords and rushed at each other like two wild bulls. Striking again and again, they hewed segments of armor from each other's bodies. Each received many deep wounds. The armor of each was covered with blood. Arthur struck such a fierce blow that his sword broke at the hilt and the blade flew into three pieces. The Black Knight groaned and blindly staggered in a circle. But he soon recovered. Seeing Arthur standing nearby and not realizing that Arthur now had no sword with which to defend himself, the Black Knight threw his shield aside and, taking his sword in both hands, delivered a blow that cut

through Arthur's helmet to his skull. Arthur sank to his knees. From inside his helmet, blood and sweat flowed down into his eyes, blinding him. The Black Knight called on Arthur to yield and surrender his shield. Arthur grabbed hold of the Black Knight's sword belt and lifted himself to his feet. Then he threw his arms around the Black Knight and, placing his knee behind the Black Knight's thigh, threw him backward onto the ground. The Black Knight lost consciousness. Arthur unlaced the Black Knight's helmet and looked at his face. Arthur immediately recognized his opponent as King Pellinore, who had warred against him twice and whom Arthur had driven into the forest.

As soon as Pellinore regained consciousness, Arthur said, "Yield, Sir Pellinore! You're at my mercy." Arthur held a dagger to Pellinore's throat. Pellinore saw blood flowing heavily from under Arthur's helmet. He caught Arthur by the wrist and directed the point of the dagger away from his own throat. Arthur felt faint from loss of blood. Pellinore heaved himself up from the ground, threw Arthur, and kneeled on top of him. He wrenched the dagger from Arthur's hand and began to unlace Arthur's helmet, intending to slay Arthur where he lay. Merlin hurried forward, crying, "Stop! Stop, Sir Pellinore! Don't commit sacrilege. The man who lies beneath you is Arthur, king of Britain!"

Astonished, Pellinore paused. Then he bellowed, "Do you say so, old man? In that case your words have doomed him to death because he has caused me great harm. He has robbed me of my kingship, honors, and estates, leaving me only this dismal forest castle. He's in my power now. If I let him go, he'll take revenge on me when he recovers. No. He'll die at my hands."

"He won't because I'll save him!" Merlin declared. With his staff he struck Pellinore across the shoulders. Pellinore fell to the ground face down.

Arthur raised himself on his elbow and saw

Pellinore lying as if dead. "Merlin, what have you done?" he cried. "You've killed one of the world's best knights!"

"Not so, my lord," Merlin said. "You're much nearer to death than he is. He'll soon regain consciousness, but you may die of your wounds."

Arthur was indeed grievously wounded. With great difficulty Merlin helped him up onto his horse. Merlin hung Arthur's shield on the horn of his saddle. Leading Arthur's horse by the bridle, Merlin conveyed Arthur across the bridge and into the forest. A holy hermit lived nearby. He was so gentle that wild birds would come and rest on his hand while he read his breviary. Sometimes nobles visited him for his blessing. Merlin conveyed Arthur to the hermit's hut.

The hermit expressed pity and sorrow at Arthur's condition. He and Merlin lifted Arthur from his saddle and carried him into the hut. They laid Arthur on a moss pallet, unlaced his armor, and bathed and dressed his wounds. For the rest of that day and part of the next, Arthur lay near death. His vision was blurry, his breathing weak. He couldn't lift his head.

On the afternoon of the second day Lady Guinevere of Cameliard and her court of ladies and knights came to the hermit on a pilgrimage. Guinevere had a favorite page who was very sick with a fever. She believed that the hermit could give her a charm that would cure the page. Guinevere saw Merlin standing beside the hut's door and Arthur's white horse eating grass in the nearby glade. "Whose horse is that?" she asked Merlin.

"A knight who is lying inside, so badly wounded that he might die."

"Heaven have pity!" Guinevere exclaimed. "My physician is very skilled at healing wounds. Maybe he can help." Guinevere entered the hut and saw Arthur lying on the pallet. She didn't know who he was, but she thought he was the noblest-looking knight she'd ever seen.

Arthur looked at Guinevere, who stood beside him surrounded by her maidens. Tall and straight, she outshone all the other women in beauty. Arthur thought that maybe he was seeing an angel who had descended from heaven to comfort him in his pain and distress. Guinevere asked her physician to dress Arthur's wounds with balsam. The ointment greatly reduced Arthur's pain. When Guinevere and her court departed, Arthur was feeling much better. Three days later he had entirely healed.

Chapter 7

On the morning of the fourth day, Arthur and Merlin walked along the forest's edge, listening to birds' cheerful singing. Arthur said, "Merlin, it greatly bothers me that Pellinore defeated me. He's the best knight I've ever encountered. Still, the outcome might have been different if my sword hadn't broken and left me defenseless. I want to fight him again as soon as possible."

"Given how close you were to death only a few days ago, you certainly are brave," Merlin said. "But you have no sword, spear, or dagger."

"I'll look for a weapon," Arthur said. "I want to fight Pellinore again even if I have to use a wooden club."

"Since you're so determined, I'll do everything I can to help you," Merlin said. "Not far from here there's an enchanted land with a large lake. A woman's arm rises from the lake's center. The arm is beautiful and dressed in white silk. It holds a sword, of unequalled brightness and beauty, called Excalibur. Several knights and numerous other people have tried to obtain Excalibur. No one has been able to touch it, and many have died trying. When anyone approaches Excalibur, either that person sinks into the lake or the arm disappears. I can lead you to the lake. When you see Excalibur, you'll want to acquire it. If you succeed, you'll have a sword fit for any battle."

"Lead me there," Arthur said.

After receiving the hermit's blessing, Merlin and Arthur left for the enchanted lake. Within the forest they saw a white doe with a gold collar. "Look, Merlin," Arthur said. "Let's follow that beautiful doe." The doe turned, and Arthur and Merlin followed her to a small opening of soft, sweet grass. They saw a table in front of a chamber. The table was spread with a white cloth and set with wine, white bread, and several types of meat. A black-haired, black-eyed page dressed in green stood at the chamber's entrance. "King Arthur, you're welcome here," he said. "Please dismount and refresh yourself."

Arthur was astonished that the page knew him. He wondered whether any magic was involved that might harm him. "Lord, you can freely partake of this refreshment, which was prepared especially for you," Merlin said. Reassured, Arthur sat down at the table. The black-haired page and another like him served Arthur food on silver plates and wine in gold goblets. After eating his fill, Arthur washed his hands in a silver basin that the first page gave him and wiped them on a fine linen napkin that the second page brought him. Merlin, too, had refreshed himself. The two went their way.

Mid-afternoon Arthur and Merlin emerged from the forest onto a plain with many beautiful flowers. The air was so radiant that it seemed to be of gold. Here and there on the plain were blossoming trees whose fragrance was sweeter than any Arthur ever had smelled before. Birds of many colors were in the trees, singing beautiful melodies. In the middle of the plain was a lake as bright as silver and bordered with lilies and daffodils. There was no sign of human life. Wondering what strange things were about to happen, Arthur led his white horse through the long grass.

When he reached the lake's edge, Arthur saw the arm in the middle of the lake. Motionless, the arm was encircled with several bracelets of finely crafted gold. It held aloft a magnificent sword. The sun shone on the sword's hilt, which was gold set with jewels. Arthur sat on his horse, marveling. He didn't know how he would get to the sword because the lake was very wide and deep. Suddenly a lady approached through the tall flowers that bloomed along the lake's shores. Arthur dismounted and went forward to meet

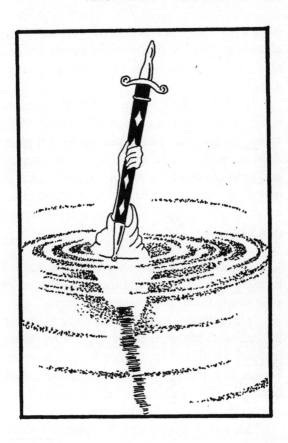

her. She was extraordinarily beautiful, with completely clear skin and black eyes that glistened like two jewels set in ivory. Her hair was black, silky, and so long that it reached the ground. She was dressed all in green, except that a cord of crimson and gold was woven into her braided hair. She wore a necklace and bracelets of opals and emeralds set in gold. Arthur kneeled before her and said, "I can see that you're no mortal woman but a fairy."

The lady replied, "King Arthur, I am indeed a fairy. I'm Nymue, the Lady of the Lake. What appears to you as a lake is actually a flowery plain. A white marble castle adorned with ultramarine and gold stands in the middle of that plain. To prevent mortals from viewing our dwelling-place, my sisters and I have hidden it behind the illusion of a lake."

"I fear that I've intruded," Arthur said.

"No, you're very welcome here. I feel much friendliness toward you and the noble knights of your court. What brings you here?"

"I recently was badly wounded in a fight with Sir Pellinore. My spear shattered, and my sword snapped. I even lost my dagger. I need a weapon. Merlin told me about Excalibur. I came here hoping to obtain that excellent sword so that I can complete my combat with Sir Pellinore."

"My lord," Nymue said, "no man can obtain Excalibur unless he's fearless and beyond reproach."

"That's sad news for me," Arthur said. "Although I don't lack courage, there are many things about which I reproach myself. Still, I'd like to attempt this even if doing so places me in great danger. Please tell me how to undertake this."

Nymue blew into an emerald whistle that hung from a small gold chain at her waist. A brass boat appeared far off on the lake and sped forward. Its prow was shaped like a woman's head. The boat had one swan-like wing on each side and moved on the water like a swan. The long lines of its wake looked like silver threads. Otherwise the water was as smooth as glass. The boat pulled up to the shore, and Nymue invited Arthur to board. As soon as he did, the boat moved swiftly across the lake to the uplifted arm. Nymue and Merlin remained on shore, gazing after the boat.

Arthur reached out and took Excalibur in his hand. The arm disappeared beneath the water. Arthur's heart swelled with joy. Excalibur was a hundred times more beautiful than he had thought possible. The boat quickly bore him back to land. When he stepped ashore, Arthur thanked Nymue for her aid. He and Merlin mounted their horses and rode away.

About noon the next day, they reached Pellinore's valley. "Merlin," Arthur said, "this time I strictly forbid you to interfere. I forbid you to use magic in my behalf." Arthur rode onto the bridge, seized the brass hammer, and struck the black shield with all his might. Pellinore came out. Arthur said, "Sir Pellinore, we have a quarrel with each other. You object to my having taken your kingly estate away and driven you into this forest solitude, although I had good reasons for doing so. I object to your affronting and injuring lords, knights, and others of my kingdom. Therefore, I challenge you to fight me until one of us has conquered the other."

Pellinore bowed his head in agreement. He wheeled his horse around, rode a small distance away, and took up his position. Arthur, too, got into position. A page from the castle gave Arthur a stout spear of ash. When the two knights were ready, they shouted and drove their horses together. They struck each other so soundly that their spears shattered. Arthur and Pellinore jumped from their horses, drew their swords, and fell to furious combat. Having Excalibur, Arthur gave Pellinore several wounds and received none. Pellinore's armor soon was covered with blood. Finally Arthur delivered such a powerful blow that it numbed Pellinore. Pellinore's sword and shield fell down, his legs trembled, and he sank to his knees. "Spare my life, and I'll yield to you," he said.

"I'll do more than spare you," Arthur said. "Because you've yielded, I'll give you back your power and estates. I bear you no ill will. But I'll tolerate no rebels against my authority. As God is my judge, I act in my people's best interests. Whoever is against me is also against them. However, now that you've acknowledged me as your superior, I'll take you into my favor. As a

pledge of your good faith, send me your two old-
est sons, Sir Aglaval and Sir Lamorack. You may
keep your youngest son, Dornar, with you as a
comfort." Pellinore agreed.

Arthur and Pellinore went into Pellinore's
castle, where Pellinore's wounds were dressed
and he was made comfortable. That night Arthur
stayed in the castle. The next morning he and
Merlin headed back to the royal court, which
awaited Arthur in the forest.

Arthur and Merlin delighted in riding through
the forest. The woods were decked in bright
green. Each thicket was full of perfume. Birds sang
within every tangled depth, as if their little throats
would burst with melody. The horses stepped
silently because the ground beneath their feet was
so soft with fragrant moss. Bright yellow sunlight
came down through the leaves, producing many
trembling circles of light on the ground. When the
sunlight shone on Arthur, his armor seemed to
catch fire with glory.

Arthur rejoiced that he had converted
Pellinore from a bitter enemy to an ally and that
he had obtained Excalibur, which hung by his
side. "Lord, which would you rather have:
Excalibur or its sheath?" Merlin asked.

"Ten thousand times over, I'd rather have
Excalibur," Arthur answered.

"You're wrong to feel that way," Merlin said.
"Excalibur's tempered steel can cut an iron bar in

two, but its sheath protects its wearer from being wounded in battle or losing even a single drop of blood. As you know, you suffered no wound in your last combat with Sir Pellinore."

Arthur frowned. "Then, there was no glory in my defeating him. A knight doesn't deserve any credit unless he fights by means of his own strength, not by magic. I've half a mind to return to the magic lake and throw Excalibur back in."

"My lord, what you say is right with regard to ordinary knights. However, you're a king. Your life doesn't belong to you but to your people. You should do everything possible to preserve your life. Keep Excalibur so that it can protect you."

Arthur considered. "You're right, Merlin. For my people's sake I'll keep Excalibur and its sheath. Since God saw fit to entrust me with such a marvelous sword, he must have ordained great things for me. I'll treasure Excalibur and use it only in God's service."

Arthur had a box made for Excalibur. He wrapped the sword in fine linen and placed it inside on a crimson silk cushion. The box was locked with three large padlocks. People never saw Excalibur except when it shone like a flame in battle.

Chapter 8

Arthur invited many nobles to a feast at his castle. Seven kings, five queens, sixty-seven lords and ladies, and many famous knights came together in good fellowship. When Arthur looked around him and saw peace and goodwill where there previously had been conflict and ill regard, he was greatly pleased.

During the feast a messenger came from the west. "My lord king, I come from King Leodegrance of Cameliard," he said to Arthur. "King Ryence of North Wales threatens to wage war on my master unless my master meets two demands. King Leodegrance no longer has many knights at his service. Since you, in your majesty, brought peace to this realm and reduced the power of all the kings under you, knights who once made my master's court famous have gone elsewhere, seeking combat opportunities. Therefore my master requests aid from you, his king."

Arthur's face darkened. "I'm sorry to hear this news. I'll quickly aid your master. What has

King Ryence demanded?"

"He has demanded that my master give him much of Cameliard that borders North Wales. He also has demanded that my master's daughter, Lady Guinevere, marry King Ryence's cousin Duke Mordaunt of North Umber. Although he's a mighty warrior, Duke Mordaunt is very ugly and has a violent temper."

Arthur angrily left the banquet hall and went to a private room, where he paced. No one dared to disturb him. He hadn't forgotten Guinevere's kindness and beauty. It sickened him to think that she might be forced to marry Mordaunt. After some time Arthur summoned Merlin, Ulfius, and Kay. He consulted with them for a considerable time. Arthur then instructed Merlin to prepare to accompany him on a journey. He commanded Ulfius and Kay to immediately gather a large army and bring it to the royal castle of Tintagel, near the borders of North Wales and Cameliard.

The next day Arthur, Merlin, and Arthur's best warriors—Gawain, Ewaine, Pellias, and Geraint—set out for Tintagel. After one and a half days they reached that large, regal castle. Arthur was received with great rejoicing because he was much loved.

The next morning, before the summer's heat was great, Arthur and Merlin walked in the garden. All around were shade-giving trees in which birds sang sweetly. Arthur said, "Merlin, I think

Lady Guinevere is the most beautiful lady in the world. I constantly think of her, whether I'm eating, drinking, walking, sitting, or attending to business. I also often dream of her at night. I've loved her ever since I met her a month ago, when I lay near death in the hermit's hut. She stood beside my bed like a shining angel. I'm not willing to let any other man marry her. I know that your magical powers include the ability to give a man a new appearance so that no one recognizes him. Please do that with me. I wish to go, disguised, to Cameliard, where I can observe Lady Guinevere every day without her knowing my feelings for her and where I can assess the dangers confronting my good friend King Leodegrance."

"My lord," Merlin said, "I'll disguise you so well that no one in the world will recognize you." Later that morning Merlin brought Arthur a small cap. As soon as Arthur put it on, his appearance changed to that of a peasant. Arthur commanded that a jacket of coarse wool be brought to him. He put the jacket on over his royal clothes, hiding the gold necklace and jewel pendant that he always wore around his neck. Disguised in this way he set out by foot for Cameliard.

As sunset approached, Arthur reached Cameliard, a town of many attractive houses with red walls and shining windows. The houses all sat on a steep hill. A high, strong wall encircled the town, which was guarded by a great castle with many towers and roofs. Beautiful gardens, lawns, meadows, orchards, and groves surrounded the castle. A flaming sunset lit the sky behind the castle, silhouetting its towers, roofs, and chimneys. Great flocks of pigeons circled the towers. Arthur thought he never had seen such a pleasing place.

At the castle, Arthur asked the head gardener for a job gardening near Guinevere's rooms. Because Arthur was tall, strong, and well built, the gardener hired him. In that pleasant summer season Guinevere and her ladies walked among the flowers every day, so Arthur was able to observe her often. He worked in the castle garden for more than a week.

One early morning while it was still cool, one of Guinevere's ladies, Mellicene, opened a window and looked out over the rose garden adjoining Guinevere's chamber. In the garden was a marble statue of a youth holding a pitcher. Crystal-clear water flowed from the pitcher into a marble basin. Because the statue stood in the shadow of a linden tree surrounded by a thick growth of roses, it could be seen only by someone looking out from the windows above. As she looked out, Mellicene saw Arthur kneeling beside the fountain washing his face and chest. Sunlight shone on him through the linden tree's leaves. His hair and beard were reddish gold. His brow, throat, and chest were as white as alabaster. His beautiful gold necklace hung around his neck. Mellicene stood entranced with wonder and pleasure. She quietly left the window and ran down the tower stairs, through the garden, and to the fountain.

Hearing her coming, Arthur quickly put his magic cap back on. When Mellicene arrived, he again looked like a laborer. "Who are you?" she demanded. "Why are you sitting here by the fountain?"

"I'm the gardener's new assistant," Arthur replied.

"Who's the young knight who was here beside the fountain just now? Where did he go?"

"Lady," Arthur replied, "no one but me has been at the fountain today."

"You're lying!" Mellicene cried. "I just saw a young knight washing himself here."

"Lady, I've told you the truth," Arthur said.

Mellicene didn't know whether or not to believe him. Annoyed, she said, "If you're lying, I'll have you whipped." She turned and left. Mellicene told Guinevere what she had seen. Guinevere laughed and said that Mellicene must have been dreaming. Mellicene herself started to think the same thing. Nevertheless, she looked out of the window every morning after that, hoping to see the knight.

For some time Arthur avoided washing at the

fountain. Then he felt it was safe to wash there again. Mellicene saw him. This time she ran to Guinevere's chamber and woke her. "My lady! My lady! Come with me! The young knight I told you about is washing himself at the fountain."

Guinevere jumped out of bed and hurried to the window that overlooked the fountain. She saw Arthur put on his purple linen tunic threaded with gold. His gold necklace was lying beside the fountain. After gazing, astonished, for some time, Guinevere said to Mellicene, "Come with me." The two descended the tower stairs and hurried to the fountain. As before, Arthur had reassumed a laborer's appearance. "Where's the young knight who was at the fountain?" Guinevere demanded.

"Lady, I'm the only person who's been at the fountain this morning," Arthur said.

When Arthur had hurriedly put on his magic cap, he had forgotten his gold necklace. Guinevere saw it still lying beside the fountain. "What's this, then?" she questioned. "Since when do gardeners wear gold necklaces? You deserve to be whipped for lying to me. Take the necklace back to its owner, and tell him from me that it ill becomes him to secretly visit a lady's private gardens." Guinevere turned and left.

As she embroidered that day, Guinevere kept wondering how the young knight could vanish so quickly. Then she had an idea. In the late afternoon she instructed Mellicene to tell the gardener's assistant to bring her a basket of fresh roses. Arthur soon brought the roses. He wore his cap in Guinevere's presence. When Guinevere's ladies saw this apparent impertinence, they cried out against Arthur. Mellicene said, "How dare you stand in front of the princess without taking your cap off! Take it off this instant!"

Arthur replied, "Lady, I can't."

"Why not?" Guinevere demanded."

"I have an ugly place on my head," Arthur said.

Guinevere snatched the cap from Arthur's head. He instantly changed from a gardener to a knight. All of the ladies stared in amazement. Some of them shrieked. Arthur dropped the basket of roses. Flowers fell all over the floor. Guinevere recognized Arthur as the knight who had lain badly wounded in the hermit's hut. She laughed, flung Arthur his cap, and mocked, "Take your cap and go your way, gardener with an ugly place on your head."

Saying nothing, Arthur somberly put the cap on, reassuming the humble guise of a gardener. He turned and left, leaving the roses where they had fallen. Guinevere instructed her ladies to say nothing of the incident.

Chapter 9

King Leodegrance received word that King Ryence and Duke Mordaunt were coming, accompanied by many knights and lords. This news caused Leodegrance fear.

When Ryence and Mordaunt appeared before the castle, Leodegrance went out to greet them. He welcomed them and invited them into the castle for refreshment and entertainment. Ryence replied, "We aren't such good friends of yours that we care to sit down at your table. In fact, we're your enemies until you agree to give me the lands that I've demanded and also agree to the marriage of Lady Guinevere and my cousin Duke Mordaunt. We'll stay here outside your castle for five days awaiting your answer, which will determine whether we're your friends or enemies."

"Meanwhile," Mordaunt said, "I'm ready to fight any knight of your court who contests my right to marry Lady Guinevere. If you have no knight who can defeat me in combat, you hardly can hope to defeat the great army of knights that

King Ryence has gathered to fight you if you deny what we ask."

Leodegrance silently turned away and walked back into his castle. Ryence, Mordaunt, and their court of lords and knights pitched their pavilions in the meadows around Leodegrance's castle. The pavilions covered the plain. Ryence and his followers feasted, sang, and made merry.

The next morning Mordaunt, in full armor, rode up and down in front of the castle. "Knights of Cameliard," he challenged, "is there no one among you willing to fight me? How, then, can you hope to defeat the knights of North Wales?" No one in Leodegrance's court was equal to Mordaunt in strength, skill, and bravery, so no one came forward to fight him. Many people gathered on the castle walls and gazed down on Mordaunt. All felt grief and shame that there was no one in Cameliard to accept his challenge. The lords and knights of Ryence's court laughed, clapped, and cheered Mordaunt.

Still disguised as a laborer, Arthur went into the town of Cameliard to see the merchant Ralph of Cardiff, known far and wide for his great wealth. Before entering Ralph's house, Arthur took off his magic cap and returned to his noble appearance. Inside, he showed Ralph his signet ring, which the merchant recognized as the ring of the king of Britain.

"Sir Merchant," Arthur said, "you no doubt

know that Duke Mordaunt continually rides up and down in front of King Leodegrance's castle, challenging anyone to fight him in behalf of Lady Guinevere. I intend to accept Duke Mordaunt's challenge. I hope to uphold the honor of Cameliard and bring shame on its enemies. I've heard that you own several suits of superb armor. I wish to buy the best one and wear it to fight Duke Mordaunt."

"My lord," Ralph said, "I'll gladly provide you with the armor. I'm grateful that you'll fight the duke." He rang a small silver bell, and several servants appeared. Ralph instructed them to provide the king with every honor and comfort. Arthur was bathed in warm, perfumed water and wiped with soft linen towels. Then he was led to a table in a hall hung with tapestries. Ralph himself served Arthur various meats, fine white bread, and ruby-red and golden wine. When Arthur had eaten his fill, six pages dressed in sky-blue silk took him to a magnificent suite where they dressed him in a padded shirt of white satin and, over that, Spanish armor inlaid with gold. They gave him a shield of pure white. The servants then conducted Arthur to the courtyard. There stood a white horse with trappings of pure white. The bridle and rein were studded all over with silver bosses. Arthur mounted. Ralph offered him many good wishes. Arthur bid Ralph goodbye and rode away, all shining in white and silver. As Arthur rode down the town's narrow, stony streets, people turned and gazed after him.

Arthur headed to the castle's back gate, where he dismounted and tied his horse. He entered the garden and told a servant that he wished to speak to Lady Guinevere. The servant, amazed at Arthur's lordly presence, delivered the message. Wondering, Guinevere hurried down a gallery and emerged at a place above Arthur. When Arthur looked up and saw her, he was struck anew by her beauty. "Lady," he said, "I'm determined to honor you as much as I can. I'm going to fight Duke Mordaunt. I believe that I'll defeat him. Before I go, I ask you for some token that I can carry or wear as your knight."

Guinevere said, "Sir Knight, I don't know who you are, but I accept you as my champion. What would you like as a token?"

"May I have your pearl necklace to wear around my arm? I believe that would inspire me to great valor."

"You shall have it," Guinevere answered. She took the necklace from her long, smooth neck and dropped it down to Arthur. He tied the necklace around his arm. Arthur thanked and saluted Guinevere with great grace. She saluted him in return. Joyful, Arthur rode away.

Word quickly spread that a knight was going to fight Mordaunt. Leodegrance, Guinevere, and their entire court came to the castle walls that overlooked the place where the combat would take place. The castle's gate was raised; the bridge was dropped; and Arthur, identified only as the White Knight, rode out to meet Mordaunt. As Arthur rode over the narrow bridge, his horse's hooves loudly struck the boards. In the sunlight Arthur's armor flashed like lightning. The people cheered when they saw him. Mordaunt rode up to Arthur and said, "Sir, there is no coat of arms on your helmet or shield, so I don't know who you are. But you must be a knight of good quality and proven courage."

"Sir Knight," Arthur said, "my quality equals yours, and my courage has been demonstrated in many encounters."

"You speak with much spirit," Mordaunt said, "but it's time for you to pray. I'll throw you from your horse so that you'll never rise again. I've defeated better men than you."

Arthur calmly replied, "The outcome will be according to God's will, not yours."

Arthur and Mordaunt saluted each other, rode to their places, and prepared their spears and shields. Silence fell on the gathering. Arthur and Mordaunt sat like iron statues. Then, shouting and spurring their horses, they launched forward. Arthur and Mordaunt met mid-course with a noise like a thunderclap. Mordaunt's spear shattered, leaving only a remnant. Arthur's spear remained intact. Mordaunt was hurled from his

saddle. He whirled in the air and fell to the ground with a great clang.

Everyone on the castle wall cheered. Members of Ryence's court ran to Mordaunt where he lay on the ground. They unlaced his helmet to give him air. Mordaunt was unconscious but alive. For some time Arthur remained seated on his horse, watching. Then, amid the rejoicing of Leodegrance's people, he rode off into the countryside. Because he expected more trouble from Mordaunt, he thought it best not to reveal his identity yet.

Arthur found the day extraordinarily sweet and pleasant. Bright clouds swam across the blue sky. The wind blew across the meadow's long grass and the fields of growing wheat, producing a sea of waves. Birds sang gaily in the hedgerows and leafy thickets. With the visor of his helmet raised so that he could feel the gentle breeze on his face, Arthur sang as he traveled.

Arthur came to a tall, handsome tower on a green hillock by the road. Three lovely young women, dressed in green silk, stood on the balcony. A knight sat on a horse on the highroad in front of the tower. He played a lute and sang sweetly. The ladies listened, continually clapping and asking for more. The sight pleased Arthur. As he approached, he recognized the knight as his friend Sir Geraint, who had accompanied him from Camelot to Tintagel. Arthur laughed to himself and closed his visor.

When Geraint saw Arthur approaching, he stopped singing and swung his lute over his shoulder. Looking up at the three young women, he said, "Ladies, you've been pleased to listen to the singing that I've undertaken in your honor. Also in your honor I'll now throw that approaching knight."

"Sir Knight," one lady said, "your bearing is noble, and you speak pleasantly. We wish you success."

Geraint thanked the three ladies and closed his helmet's visor. He prepared his spear and shield, saluted the three ladies, and went forward to meet Arthur, who sat waiting. Geraint didn't recognize Arthur, whose helmet and shield had no coat of arms. "Sir," Geraint said, "I don't know who you are. However, I wish to honor the three ladies on that balcony by jousting with you. I'm ready to defend my claim that those ladies are more beautiful than your lady, whoever she may be."

"Sir Knight," Arthur said, "I'll gladly joust with you in honor of my lady, who is a princess and widely considered to be the most beautiful woman in the world. But I'll contend with you only on this condition: whichever one of us is thrown will serve the other for seven days, doing whatever is required of him."

"I agree," Geraint said. "When I've thrown you, I'll turn you over to those three ladies to be their servant for seven days. Many knights would regard that as a pleasant and honorable task."

"If I throw you," Arthur replied, "I'll send you to serve my lady for seven days. That will be an even more pleasant and honorable task."

Arthur and Geraint saluted each other and took up their positions. After both had prepared and sat still for a brief period, they rushed forward. They met directly below the balcony from which the three ladies were watching. Geraint's spear shattered. Arthur's remained intact. Geraint was thrown backwards so violently that he and his horse fell to the ground. When

Geraint had recovered his footing, he stood in astonishment. He never had been thrown before. Drawing his sword, he vehemently demanded that Arthur dismount and fight him on foot.

"No," Arthur said. "I've thrown you, so you must keep your promise and do as I say for seven days."

Ashamed and annoyed, Geraint realized that he must honor his promise, so he put his sword away. "I yield to your commands, according to my promise."

"Go now to Lady Guinevere at Cameliard," Arthur said. "Tell her that the knight to whom she gave her pearl necklace has thrown you and that you'll obey her commands for seven days."

"I'll do as you say," Geraint said. He mounted his horse and rode away. Arthur, too, rode off. The ladies on the balcony were delighted to have witnessed such an exciting contest.

After some time Arthur came to a marsh with several windmills whose sails slowly turned in the wind. There was a long, straight causeway with willows down each side. Arthur saw two knights sitting in the shade of a large windmill on one side of the causeway. They were eating white cheese and a loaf of bread that the miller had served them. When the two knights saw Arthur, they stopped eating and closed their helmets. Knowing that a joust would follow, the miller quickly went back into his mill and shut the door.

He looked down on the knights from a window.

Arthur chuckled to himself when he saw that the two knights were his nephews Gawain and Ewaine. At some distance he closed his helmet so that they wouldn't recognize him. Gawain rode forward to meet Arthur. "Sir Knight," Gawain said, "you've ventured onto perilous ground. There's no way across the marsh except forward, and you can't go forward without jousting with me."

"Sir Knight," Arthur said, "I'm very willing to joust with you, but only on one condition: whichever one of us is thrown will serve the other for seven days."

Confident of winning, Gawain agreed to Arthur's terms. When the two knights clashed, Arthur knocked Gawain off his horse. Gawain fell with such violence that he lay dazed for a time. "I've thrown you," Arthur said. "Now you must keep your promise."

"Not so fast," Ewaine said. "I demand that you joust with me and that if I throw you, you release my cousin from the seven days of service. If you throw me, I'll serve you for the same seven days."

"I accept your challenge," Arthur said.

Arthur and Ewaine came at each other like two rams on a hillside. Ewaine's saddle straps burst, and he fell from his horse with great force. He got up and stood looking at Arthur with amazement. "You, too, must keep your promise," Arthur said. "I command you to do the same thing as your cousin: serve Lady Guinevere for seven days."

"We'll do as you've commanded," Gawain said. "But when the seven days are up, I'll seek you out and continue this combat. Any knight can be thrown one time. I believe I'll overcome you in further battle."

"As you wish. However, I think that when the seven days are up, you no longer will want to fight me." Arthur saluted his nephews, they saluted him, and Arthur rode off. His nephews' astonishment and chagrin made him laugh out loud.

When Ewaine had mended his saddle straps, he and Gawain headed for Cameliard. The miller was delighted to have safely witnessed the jousting.

Late in the afternoon Arthur saw a gnarled, stunted oak tree ahead. A shield hung on the tree. These words were written underneath the shield in large letters: "Whoever strikes this shield does so at his peril." Arthur struck the shield with his spear so that the shield rang like thunder. Dressed all in white and riding a white horse with white trappings, a large knight quickly approached Arthur. The emblem on his helmet was a swan with outspread wings. His shield showed three swans. Arthur recognized the knight as Sir Pellias, who had accompanied him from Camelot to Tintagel.

Pellias came up to Arthur and sternly said,

"Sir Knight, why did you strike my shield? That blow will bring you danger and sorrow. Prepare to defend yourself." Arthur then exacted the same pledge from Pellias that he had exacted from Geraint, Gawain, and Ewaine. Arthur and Pellias came together with the force of two stones hurled from a catapult. Pellias was thrown from his horse. Arthur waited beside him a considerable time, until Pellias was able to rise. Arthur then ordered Pellias to go to Lady Guinevere and deliver the same message as that of Geraint, Gawain, and Ewaine. "I'll do as you command," Pellias said, "but I wish I knew your identity. No one ever has thrown me with such force."

"Some time you'll know who I am," Arthur said. "For now, I'm bound to secrecy." He saluted Pellias and rode into the forest. Dejected and wondering, Pellias rode off toward Cameliard.

So that day Geraint, Gawain, Ewaine, and Pellias all appeared before Guinevere. They were very embarrassed to see one another under these circumstances. When they conveyed Arthur's message, Guinevere was proud that her champion had defeated such famous knights. She was very glad that she had given her pearl necklace to such a worthy knight, who had done her such honor. She longed to know his identity.

Chapter 10

Mordaunt fully recovered from the wounds he had suffered at Arthur's hands. In full armor he returned to the meadow in front of the castle at Cameliard. Two heralds accompanied him, blowing trumpets. Many people gathered on the castle walls. Leodegrance stood on a tower that looked down on Mordaunt, who looked up and shouted, "King Leodegrance, don't think that you're rid of me simply because I fell from my horse due to a mischance. Tomorrow I'll come here with six other knights. If you have seven knights who can defeat my companions and me in combat by sunset tomorrow—with spears or swords, on horses or on foot—I'll drop my claim to Lady Guinevere's hand. Otherwise I'll not only claim Lady Guinevere; I'll also seize your three castles on North Umber's borders and all the lands around those castles." Mordaunt rode away.

Leodegrance felt despair. He thought, "I'm extremely unlikely to find others like that wonderful White Knight. Where has he gone? I wish

I could ask him for further aid." Leodegrance went to his private chamber, where he grieved, refusing to speak to anyone.

Guinevere now thought of the four knights who had pledged to serve her for seven days. "Sirs," she said to them, "I charge you to accept Duke Mordaunt's challenge. Tomorrow meet him and his knight companions in combat. You're wonderfully strong men. I believe you'll easily defeat our enemies."

Gawain said, "Lady, although we've pledged to serve you, we haven't pledged to serve your father. We have no quarrel with Duke Mordaunt or his six companions. We're King Arthur's knights; we can't serve any other king without his permission."

Angry, Guinevere said, "Either you're wonderfully faithful to your king, Sir Gawain, or you're afraid to fight Duke Mordaunt and his knights."

Guinevere's words infuriated Gawain. "If you were a knight, Lady Guinevere, you'd think twice before speaking to me so disrespectfully." He rose and left. Guinevere went to her chamber, where she wept with anger and worry.

Arthur secretly approached one of Guinevere's pages. Pulling Guinevere's pearl necklace from his jacket, Arthur instructed the page, "Take this necklace to Lady Guinevere. Tell her that I, the White Knight, want her to send me

Sir Gawain, Sir Ewaine, Sir Geraint, and Sir Pellias. They should be dressed for battle. I'll be waiting outside the castle's back gate. Also tell Lady Guinevere that she should command them to do whatever I command."

When Guinevere received her pearl necklace and Arthur's message, she was overjoyed at the White Knight's return. She went to the four knights and said, "My lords, when I commanded you to do combat with Duke Mordaunt, you refused. You, Sir Gawain, spoke angry words unsuited to one serving his mistress, let alone a princess. If you're to keep the pledge you made to my champion, the White Knight, you now will do as I command. Put on your full battle gear. Go to the White Knight, who is waiting outside the castle's back gate. Do whatever he commands."

The four knights did as commanded. Dressed for battle, they went to Arthur, who raised his visor, revealing his identity. Geraint, Gawain, Ewaine, and Pellias were silent and motionless with astonishment. "No greeting for me?" Arthur said merrily, enjoying their amazement. The four knights cried out and fell to their knees before their king. Arthur bade them rise and told them everything that had happened. They were overjoyed.

The next day seven heralds with trumpets appeared on the field in front of Cameliard's castle. Seven squires rode behind them, each bearing the spear, shield, and banner of the knight who was his master. The heralds blew their trumpets so loudly that the sound reached Cameliard's farthest regions. People came running from every direction. While the heralds trumpeted, the squires shouted and waved their spears and banners. Finally Mordaunt and his six knights rode up. They paraded up and down the length of the field three times. Meanwhile a great crowd stood on the castle's walls and gazed at the spectacle. Ryence's entire court came and stood on the plain in front of his pavilion. They cheered Mordaunt and his six knights.

Leodegrance was too ashamed and troubled to show his face. He remained in his private chamber. Guinevere went there and knocked on the door. When the king refused to let her in, she spoke to him through the door. "Father, take cheer. The glorious White Knight who came to our aid surely will come again today. He'll overcome our enemies."

Without opening the door Leodegrance replied, "Daughter, I believe you're saying that only to comfort me."

"No," Guinevere said, "God is going to help us through a worthy champion."

The morning and early afternoon passed without anyone's coming to fight Mordaunt and his six companions. Several hours before sundown a cloud of dust appeared at a distance. Five knights approached at a gallop. Appearing as the

White Knight, Arthur rode foremost. Gawain, Ewaine, Geraint, and Pellias followed close behind. The people on the castle walls cheered. Leodegrance came out to see what was happening. When Guinevere saw the White Knight and his companions, she laughed and wept with joy. She waved her handkerchief at the five champions and kissed her hand to them. They saluted her as they rode past and into the field.

Mordaunt and his knight companions rode to meet their opponents. "Sir Knight," Mordaunt said to Arthur, "I previously condescended to do battle with you, even though no one here knows who you are. You threw me purely by chance. My companions and I won't fight you and your companions until we know your ranks and identities. Declare who you are."

Gawain raised his helmet's visor. "I'm Gawain, King Lot's son. My rank and estate surpass yours. As for the White Knight, he's the one who condescends when you and he do battle. His rank and merit exceed yours."

"Oh, really?" Mordaunt replied. "Few people are so exalted that they can condescend to me. Nevertheless, I'll accept your vouching for the White Knight. However, we still can't fight you because there are only five of you and seven of us. The forces are unequal. To fight would unfairly endanger you."

Gawain smiled sarcastically. "Thank you for

your compassionate concern for our safety, but it's our choice whether or not we're willing to fight when outnumbered. In my opinion you seven are in as much danger as we five. If you weren't a knight, I'd think you were concerned about your own safety, not ours."

Mordaunt blushed with shame because it was true that he felt afraid. Each knight closed his helmet and turned his horse. Arthur and his men rode to one end of the field; Mordaunt and his men rode to the other. Arthur positioned himself with two knights on each side of him. Mordaunt had three knights on each side. The combatants prepared their spears and shields. Then Arthur and Mordaunt shouted, and the opposing sides raced toward each other. The ground thundered, and clouds of dust rose into the sky. The opponents met in the middle of the field with an uproar that could be heard a mile away. Two of Mordaunt's companions were thrown. Arthur's spear pierced Mordaunt's shield and body armor. The stroke lifted Mordaunt out of his saddle and threw him a spear's length behind his horse. Mordaunt gave a final, squeaking breath and died.

When Arthur turned around at the end of the course and saw that only four opponents still were mounted, he lifted his spear, drew rein, and said to his comrades, "I'm weary. I don't wish to fight anymore today. Engage those knights in battle while I stay here and watch."

"Lord," Arthur's companions said, "we'll do as you command."

The four knights on Mordaunt's side felt fear. Nevertheless, they prepared themselves and came forward. Gawain drove straight up to the foremost knight, the well-known champion Sir Dinador of Montcalm. Gawain lifted himself up in his stirrups and struck a blow with his sword that split Dinador's shield. Then he split Dinador's helmet. Dizzy, Dinador caught the horn of his saddle to avoid falling. Then, overcome with terror, he violently drew rein to one side and fled. Dinador's companions also fled. Arthur watched in delight as Gawain, Ewaine, Geraint, and Pellias pursued Dinador and his companions straight through Ryence's court, scattering the numerous knights and nobles. When the four had chased the fleeing knights entirely away, they returned to Arthur. The people of Cameliard cheered their five champions, who rode across the drawbridge and through the gateway into the town.

Having accomplished his purpose, Arthur returned his armor to Ralph. "Tomorrow, Sir Merchant, I'll send you two bags of gold as payment."

Ralph replied, "Lord, you needn't pay me. You've saved Cameliard."

"You must accept payment," Arthur insisted.

That night Ryence and his court took down

their pavilions and left Cameliard. With great ceremony Ryence conveyed Mordaunt's body away on a litter surrounded by lit candles. About noon of the next day a herald from Ryence appeared before Leodegrance where he sat in his hall with a number of his people. "My lord king," the herald said, "my master, King Ryence, is greatly displeased with you because your knights killed Duke Mordaunt, an excellent nobleman and King Ryence's cousin. Also, you haven't replied to my master's demands regarding certain lands bordering North Wales. So my master is greatly affronted and has told me to announce two conditions: first, you must deliver into his hands the White Knight who slew Duke Mordaunt; second, you must promise that the lands in question will presently be delivered to him."

Leodegrance rose with great dignity and said, "Sir Herald, King Ryence's demands pass all bounds for insolence. Duke Mordaunt died because of his own pride and folly. I wouldn't deliver the White Knight into your master's hands even if I could. As for the lands that King Ryence demands, tell him that I won't give him so much as a single blade of grass."

"If that's your answer, King Leodegrance, I've been instructed to tell you that King Ryence will presently come here with an army and forcibly take what you won't give him peaceably." The herald departed.

Leodegrance went to his private chamber and sent for Guinevere. He said, "Daughter, a knight dressed all in white and bearing no coat of arms has come to our rescue twice. People are saying that this knight is your personal champion and that he wore your necklace when he fought Duke Mordaunt. Please tell me who the White Knight is and where I can find him."

"I don't know who he is," Guinevere said with much regret.

Leodegrance took Guinevere's hand. "You're of an age when you should consider marrying a man who will cherish and protect you. I'm getting old. I can't defend you from the dangers that threaten us. Since King Arthur brought peace to this realm, the knights who once gathered around me have scattered. Only one knight is willing and able to defend us in these dangerous times: the White Knight. It seems to me that you couldn't hope to find anyone braver and nobler. It would be good if you felt inclined toward him; he apparently feels inclined toward you."

Guinevere blushed. Tears of joy came into her eyes. "I think I'd be pleased to marry the White Knight." Guinevere summoned Gawain, Ewaine, Pellias, and Geraint and commanded them, "Bring the White Knight here."

Arthur soon came. A cloak and large hat concealed his identity. When he stood in front of Leodegrance, he showed his face. Leodegrance cried out in amazement. "My lord and king!" Leodegrance kneeled before Arthur, who took Leodegrance's hands within his own. "Are you the White Knight?" Leodegrance asked.

"Yes," Arthur said. Stooping, he kissed Leodegrance on the cheek and lifted him to his feet. The two kings exchanged warm, complimentary words.

Guinevere was astonished. Her heart pounded. Arthur went up to her and took her by the hand. "I fear your greatness," Guinevere said.

"Lady, it is I who should fear *you*," Arthur said, "because your favor means more to me than anything else in the world. *Do* you favor me?"

"Greatly," Guinevere answered.

Arthur kissed Guinevere, sealing their betrothal. Leodegrance was overjoyed.

At Arthur's bidding, Kay and Ulfius gathered a great army. When Ryence came against Cameliard, he was completely defeated. His army scattered, and he was chased into the mountains. There was great rejoicing in Cameliard. Arthur remained there awhile with a splendid court of lords and ladies. There were feasts and many bouts at arms. Arthur and Guinevere were completely happy.

One day while he was feasting with Arthur, Leodegrance said, "My lord, what shall I offer you as a dowry when you take Guinevere as your queen?"

Arthur turned to Merlin, who stood near him. "What dowry should I ask of my friend, Merlin?"

"My lord, King Leodegrance has one thing that would greatly increase your reign's glory and renown if he bestowed it on you," Merlin said.

"What is it, Merlin?" Arthur asked.

"I had a round magical table made for your father, Uther Pendragon, during his reign. It could seat fifty knights. Whenever a seat was assigned to a knight, his name instantly appeared at his seat in gold letters. When that knight died, his name vanished. Forty-eight of the fifty seats were alike. The forty-ninth seat, set aside for the king, was raised above all the others. It was exquisitely carved, gilded, and inlaid with ivory and gold. The fiftieth seat was inlaid with silver and gold and covered with an embroidered satin canopy. No name ever appeared on this seat because only one man in the world can sit there safely. If any other man dared to sit there, he would die within three days or otherwise suffer great misfortune. During Uther's reign thirty-seven knights sat at the Round Table. Before he died, Uther bequeathed the table to King Leodegrance. At the beginning of King Leodegrance's reign, twenty-four knights sat at the table. But times have changed. The glory of King Leodegrance's reign has paled before the glory of yours, so his best knights have left his court. Today only one Round Table seat bears a name: King Leodegrance's. The table currently sits unused in a pavilion. If King Leodegrance will give you the Round Table as a dowry, your reign will achieve its greatest glory. Every seat will be filled, even the dangerous one, and the fame of the knights who sit at the Round Table never will be forgotten."

Arthur exclaimed, "The Round Table would indeed be a dowry worthy of any king!"

"Then, you shall have it," Leodegrance said. "If it brings you glory, it will bring me glory as well. After all, my daughter will be your queen."

Chapter 11

In the early fall the meadows and plains still were green. The sky still was a summer sky: light blue with large, floating clouds. Birds sang short songs in memory of spring. The air was warm, but the leaves were turning red, orange, and gold. It was very pleasant to be outdoors.

Camelot's people rejoiced that Arthur was to have a queen. Camelot was magnificently decorated in preparation for the wedding. The stony street down which Guinevere would come to the royal castle was strewn with fresh-cut rushes and covered in many places with beautifully patterned carpets. All houses along the way were hung with fine tapestries of crimson and sky blue. Flags and banners waved everywhere in the gentle breeze.

The day of the wedding was bright and clear. Arthur sat in his hall surrounded by his court, awaiting news of Guinevere's approach. Mid-morning a messenger rode up on a white horse. His pennant was set with many glistening gems. His clothes and his horse's trappings were of gold cloth embroidered with scarlet and white. The herald went to Arthur and said, "My lord king, Lady Guinevere and her court are approaching."

Arthur joyfully set out with his court of knights. They rode down the street in great state. The people cheered as Arthur passed. He smiled and bent his head from side to side in greeting. Arthur and his court rode out of the town gate and down a broad highway, lined with willows, that wound beside a shining river. Seeing Guinevere's court at a distance, they hurried forward. Guinevere's court sparkled as the sun fell on their clothes of silk and gold cloth and on their gold necklaces with hanging gems. Arthur had sent seventeen of his noblest knights, in full armor, as an escort for Guinevere. These knights rode in great splendor, surrounding the litter on which she lay. The litter's frame was of gilded wood; its curtains and cushions were of crimson silk embroidered with gold thread. Guinevere's court rode behind her litter: ladies, gentlemen, ladies-in-waiting, pages, and servants.

The courts of Arthur and Guinevere met and mingled. Arthur dismounted and walked up to Guinevere's litter while Gawain and Ewaine held his horse's bridle. A page drew aside the curtains of Guinevere's litter. Leodegrance gave Guinevere his hand, and she descended. Leodegrance led her to Arthur, who placed one hand under her chin and the other on her head and kissed her smooth cheek, which was warm, fragrant, as soft as velvet, and without blemish. Everyone cheered. In this way Arthur welcomed Guinevere and her father about a mile from Camelot's town walls.

The procession entered Camelot with great ceremony. All members were assigned apartments in the royal castle. The whole palace was alive with joy and beauty. At noon the entire court went to the cathedral, where Arthur and Guinevere were married by the archbishop. The bells rang joyfully. All the people who stood outside the cathedral cheered. Arthur and Guinevere came out all shining. He was as splendid as the sun; she was as luminous as the moon.

A great feast was held in the castle, attended by nearly five hundred royals, nobles, and knights. Leodegrance, Merlin, Ulfius, Gawain, Ewaine, Ector, Kay, and Pellinore were among the people who sat near the king and queen.

Mid-afternoon Merlin led Arthur, Guinevere, and the whole splendid court to a pavilion built partly by skill and partly by magic. When Arthur and Guinevere entered, sweet music began to play. Arthur and Guinevere were amazed at the pavilion's beauty. The walls were gilded and painted with figures of angels and saints. Dressed in ultramarine and crimson, these figures played musical instruments of gold. The pavilion's roof represented the sky; it was sky blue with an image of the sun in its center. The pavilion's floor was marble laid in squares of different colors.

"This is the Round Table!" Merlin announced. There it was in the middle of the pavilion. A gold chalice filled with fragrant wine and a gold plate with a fresh loaf of white bread were at each of the table's fifty seats. Pointing to a beautifully crafted high seat of fine, gilded wood, Merlin said, "Lord king, that's the royal seat. It's yours to sit in." KING ARTHUR suddenly appeared on the back of the seat in gold letters. "That seat may well be called the Round Table's center because you're the center of all that's most worthy and knightly." Pointing to the seat opposite the royal seat, Merlin said, "That's the dangerous seat. Only one man in the world can sit there safely, and he hasn't been born yet."

"Merlin," Arthur said, "this is marvelous. Make haste to find a sufficient number of worthy knights to fill the Round Table, so that my glory will be complete."

"Lord, you shouldn't be in such a hurry. When the Round Table's seats are filled, your glory will be at its height. From then on it will decline. In any case, we couldn't fill the Round Table now. Although you've gathered around you the noblest knights in Christendom, only thirty-one knights other than you are worthy to sit at the Round Table."

"Please point out those thirty-one," Arthur said.

Merlin looked around, saw Pellinore, and went up to him. Taking Pellinore by the hand, Merlin said to Arthur, "My lord king, with the exception of yourself this knight is the worthiest. He's gentle and generous toward the poor and needy, yet he's terribly strong and skillful." Merlin led Pellinore forward. PELLINORE appeared in gold letters on the seat just left of the royal seat. When Pellinore took his seat, all onlookers shouted acclaim.

Merlin then indicated thirty other knights in Arthur's court fit to sit at the Round Table. They included Gawain, Ewaine, Ulfius, Kay, Pellias, and Geraint. As Merlin pointed out each knight, that knight's name appeared in gold letters on his seat. When everyone had been chosen, Arthur said, "Merlin, why has the seat just right of the royal seat remained empty?"

"That seat soon will have a name on it. The man who will sit in it will be the world's greatest knight until the knight comes who will exceed all other men in handsomeness, strength, and grace and who will occupy the dangerous seat."

Surrounded by his court, the Archbishop of Canterbury went from seat to seat, blessing each one while a choir sang and attendants swung censers from which a vapor of incense ascended, filling the pavilion with fragrance. Then each knight took his seat. His squire came and stood behind him, holding a banner with the knight's coat of arms.

Then each knight rose. Holding his sword hilt in front of him, he repeated an oath spoken by King Arthur. This oath was the covenant of Round Table knighthood. Upon the cross of his sword each knight swore to be gentle toward the weak, courageous toward the strong, fierce toward evildoers, respectful of all women, merciful to all people, courteous, true in friendship, and faithful in love. The knights also pledged to defend one another and anyone helpless who asked them for aid. Having so sworn, each knight kissed the hilt of his sword. Everyone who stood watching cheered.

The knights of the Round Table seated themselves. Each broke off some bread from his loaf and drank some wine from the golden chalice that stood before him, giving thanks to God.

Chapter 12

One day Arthur, Guinevere, and their courts were happily sitting in Camelot's royal hall when an armed knight entered. His armor was covered with blood and dust. He had many wounds. Everyone present was alarmed. Nearly fainting, the knight reported that large armies of five kings—of Denmark, Ireland, Soleyse, Vale, and Longtinaise—were suddenly burning and otherwise ravaging the realm on every side.

Smiting his palms together, Arthur cried, "Oh! Will the time never come when these wars and disturbances will cease and we'll entirely have peace in this land?" He immediately sent messengers to the two friendly kings located nearest to him: Pellinore and Urien. He asked them to come to his aid. He also gathered a large army.

Two days later Arthur and his army entered the forest of Tintagel, where they awaited Pellinore's and Urien's troops. But the five kings who were Arthur's enemies learned that Arthur was in Tintagel. Before Pellinore and Urien could come to Arthur's aid, enemy troops marched through North Wales and attacked Arthur's army at night. Arthur's troops defended themselves with great spirit. Then Pellinore arrived with his army and joined in the battle. Arthur won a great victory over his enemies, who fled in every direction. As a result of his defeat of the five kings, Arthur recovered all the land that had once been his father's and more besides.

Eight knights of the Round Table died in that war. Arthur greatly mourned their loss. Merlin said to Arthur, "Don't grieve, lord. You still have many excellent knights. You can easily fill the eight places that these deaths have left vacant. Choose some worthy adviser from among the knights of the Round Table. With him, select new members."

Arthur summoned Pellinore to his private chamber and asked his opinion. Pellinore advised Arthur to select four old, wise knights and four young, ardent knights. Arthur and Pellinore chose four older knights and three younger ones. One place remained to be filled. Arthur considered two candidates. One was Sir Baudemagus, who was Ewaine's brother and the son of Urien and Morgan le Fay, Arthur's half sister. The other was Pellinore's illegitimate son Sir Tor. Because Tor was his beloved son, Pellinore declined to advise Arthur in this matter. After much consideration Arthur said, "I believe that Sir Tor is the greater knight. He already has shown himself to be a brave and able warrior. Although worthy, Sir Baudemagus hasn't yet proved himself as a soldier. Sir Tor will join the Round Table."

"So be it," Pellinore said. At that moment the names of the eight newly chosen knights appeared on seats of the Round Table.

When Queen Morgan heard the news, she was greatly affronted that her son Baudemagus hadn't been selected. She complained to her husband and sons, "How is this? Does the king care so little about birthright and kinship that he passes over his own nephew and chooses someone who isn't of lawful birth? We've suffered grievous ills at King Arthur's hands. He has taken away our royal power and made us little more than captives at his court. He has treated us like bitter enemies rather than close kin. What he now has done to Baudemagus is the greatest affront yet."

Urien rebuked his wife. He had grown to love Arthur, whom he regarded as having a noble nature. Ewaine also rebuked Morgan. "Mother, I won't hear any ill spoken of King Arthur," he said. "I love him. He epitomizes knighthood and honor." But Baudemagus shared his mother's feelings. He was angry that Arthur had passed him over. Without asking Arthur's permission, Baudemagus left Arthur's court in search of adventure. Arthur deeply regretted this.

Morgan expressed indignation to several

other people of the court, so that word of her displeasure finally reached Arthur. When Morgan came to Arthur and asked permission to leave the court, he said with much sadness, "Sister, I'm very sorry that you're displeased with my choice of a Round Table knight. I've done my best. Although I'd like Baudemagus to be a fellow of the Round Table, I truly believed that Tor had more right to a seat. If I chose a man because he's my kin, what virtue would the Round Table have?"

Morgan angrily said, "You add to the affront that our house has received at your hands. You not only deny my son that seat but also belittle him by speaking of him as inferior to the low-born knight you've chosen. The only pleasure I can have in talking to you is in asking you to let me leave here."

Arthur said with dignity, "You certainly may do as you wish. Moreover, I'll see to it that you don't leave without a court fit to accompany someone who is the wife of one king and the sister of another."

So Morgan left with great honor and in high estate. However, she still felt anger and hatred toward Arthur. At an estuary of the sea she dismissed those whom Arthur had sent with her and embarked with her own court in several ships for Avalon, the enchanted island that was her beloved home. Avalon was a paradise covered

with flower gardens and plantations of beautiful trees, some bearing fruit and others blossoms. At the island's shores, white marble terraces on smooth grass slopes overlooked the sea. Amid the gardens, orchards, and lawns were castles and towers, some as white as snow and others bright with many colors. The island's greatest marvel was a tower entirely of loadstone. That loadstone was magical. It moved Avalon from place to place in accordance with Morgan's will. No one neared Avalon without Morgan's permission. Few people had seen the island. Sometimes it was concealed behind a silvery mist of enchantment, so that only a fairy could see it. Sometimes, from a distance, people faintly heard merry voices and exquisite music coming from the island. If anyone came too close, Avalon would vanish.

Chapter 13

𝕸organ was a cunning enchantress. By means of potent spells she could work her will on all things alive or inanimate. Merlin had taught her magic while she was a young woman at King Uther's court. Except for Merlin, Morgan was the world's most powerful wizard. However, she lacked Merlin's ability to see the future.

After Morgan returned to Avalon, she brooded over what she regarded as Arthur's affront to her family. The more she brooded, the more her feeling of grievance grew. At last she felt that she couldn't be happy until she punished Arthur. Indeed, she was so angry with him that she wished him dead. Morgan knew that she couldn't harm Arthur as long as Merlin was there to protect him because Merlin would foresee any danger that might threaten the king. If she wanted to destroy Arthur, she must first destroy Merlin.

An extraordinarily beautiful young woman named Vivien resided at Morgan's court. Fifteen years old, Vivien was exceptionally cunning for her age. She also was cold and cruel to anyone who stood in the way of her getting what she wanted. Because Vivien was so cunning, Morgan liked her and taught her much sorcery. Being heartless, Vivien felt no affection for Morgan.

One day Morgan and Vivien sat together on a high terrace overlooking the sea. The day was fair and the sea so blue that it seemed as if the sky and water had melted into each other. "Vivien," Morgan said, "what thing would you most like to have?"

"Wisdom such as yours," Vivien answered.

"I know how you can be even wiser than I am," Morgan said.

"How, Lady?"

"Merlin has as much wisdom as any mortal can possess. He taught me everything I know about magic, and he knows many things that he didn't teach me. He taught me because I was beautiful. Merlin loves beauty more than anything else. He has a gift that can't be taught to anyone else: the ability to see the future. However, he can't foresee his own fate, only others'. You're far more beautiful than I was at your age, so I think you would easily attract Merlin. If I also give you a charm that I possess, Merlin will love you so much that he'll teach you more magic than he ever taught me."

"Dear lady," Vivien said, "I greatly desire to learn magic. I'll be grateful if you help me beguile Merlin so that he teaches me."

Morgan blew a small whistle of ivory and gold, and a young page came running. She commanded him to bring her a certain alabaster box that was beautifully carved, adorned with gold, and set with gems. Morgan removed two solid gold rings from the box. One was set with a brilliant diamond, the other with a blood-red ruby. "Vivien, each of these rings has magical powers. If you wear the diamond ring, whoever wears the ruby ring will love you so passionately that you can do whatever you want with him. Take these rings, go to King Arthur's court, and use them as your cunning directs." Vivien thanked Morgan and took the two rings.

At Pentecost, Arthur held a great feast. His court gathered around him with much rejoicing. Arthur sat at the table with many nobles and several kings and queens. Dressed in orange satin embroidered with silver and gold, Vivien entered the hall. Her reddish gold hair was coiled in a gold net. Her black eyes glistened. She wore a three-stranded gold necklace. She was accompanied by a dwarf also dressed in orange clothes. He carried a magnificent ruby ring on an orange silk cushion with gold tassels.

"Damsel, who are you?" Arthur asked.

"Sir, I'm Vivien, the daughter of the king of Northumberland."

"What do you have on that cushion? And

why have you honored us by coming here?"

"I've come to give you good entertainment at Pentecost," Vivien said. "Here's a ring that can be worn by only the wisest and worthiest of people."

"Show me the ring," Arthur said. Vivien brought the ring to Arthur, who picked it up. "May I put it on?"

"Yes, lord," Vivien said.

Arthur attempted to put the ring on, but it shrank to such a small size that it wouldn't go past his knuckle. "It appears that I'm not worthy to wear the ring."

"May I offer the ring to others of your court?" Vivien asked.

"Yes. Let others try."

Vivien took the ring to various lords and ladies, but no one could wear it. Finally she came to Merlin. Kneeling before him, she offered him the ring. "Child, what trick is this?" Merlin asked suspiciously.

"Sir, please try to wear this ring," Vivien said.

Merlin regarded Vivien more closely and saw that she was very beautiful. His heart softened toward her. "Why should I try on the ring?" he asked much more gently.

"I believe that you're the wisest and worthiest person here, so the ring should belong to you." Merlin smiled, took the ring, and placed it on his finger. It fit perfectly. "See!" Vivien cried.

Merlin was greatly pleased. After a while he

tried to take the ring off, but he couldn't. As if it were flesh and bone, the ring had attached to his finger. Merlin feared that the ring had magical powers. "Where does this ring come from?" he asked.

"Queen Morgan le Fay sent it."

"I hope there's no evil in it," Merlin said. The ring began to work its spell. Merlin quickly felt passionate desire for Vivien.

Seeing that the ring had worked, Vivien

laughed and turned away. Several people noticed the strange way that Merlin looked at her. "That young woman's beauty has bewitched Merlin," they said.

From then on Merlin followed Vivien wherever she went. If she was in the garden, he went there. If she was in the hall, he went there. If she went hawking, he followed on horseback. Many in the court joked about Merlin's infatuation with Vivien. She hated Merlin, whose attention annoyed her, but she behaved as if she felt great friendship toward him.

One pleasant summer day Merlin saw Vivien sitting in the garden. When he approached, she hurriedly rose to leave in order to avoid him. Merlin overtook her, saying, "Child, do you hate me?"

"No, Sir," Vivien lied.

"I love you," Merlin said. "What can I do so that you'll like me?"

"If you would teach me magic, I'd love you. As of now you're too much wiser than I am. If you would make me your equal in wisdom, we'd be better suited to each other."

"You're already wise beyond your years," Merlin said. "I fear that if I taught you magic, your knowledge would result in your undoing or mine."

"If you love me, you'll teach me magic," Vivien insisted. "Do that, and I'll love you greatly."

Although he had misgivings, Merlin said,

"I'll teach you everything you want to know."

Vivien looked down to hide her feeling of triumph. Then, raising her face, she said, "When will you teach me?"

"I can teach you only in solitude, so that nothing disturbs your study," Merlin replied. "Tomorrow tell King Arthur that you must return to your father's kingdom. You and I will leave accompanied by your court. When we've reached some secluded place, I'll build a house by means of my magic and we'll live there until I've taught you magic." Vivien took Merlin's hand and kissed it.

The next day Vivien asked Arthur to let her leave with Merlin for her father's court. Two days later she, Merlin, and a number of her servants departed. At some distance from the court of Vivien's father, Vivien and Merlin turned east toward a beautiful valley familiar to Merlin.

Chapter 14

After three days of travel Vivien, Merlin, and their attendants reached a dark forest. The trees were so thickly interwoven that nothing could be seen of the sky; their branches and roots looked like intertwined serpents. "This is a dismal woodland," Vivien said.

"Yes," Merlin said, "but the Valley of Delight is within." The travelers entered the forest. Although the day was bright, the forest was as dark as night. Many of the travelers felt afraid. Merlin encouraged them, and they continued. Much to the relief of many, the travelers soon emerged from the forest. Beneath them was a beautiful valley. In its center was a lake so clear and smooth that it looked like a silver shield. All around the lake were level meadows covered with flowers of many colors.

Vivien said to Merlin, "Master, I don't think the blessed meadows of heaven could be more beautiful than this."

As the travelers descended into the valley,

night fell. A round moon shone on the valley. Upon reaching the lake's shores, some people complained, "There's no castle or house. How will we be sheltered from rain and cold?"

Merlin overheard. "I'll provide you with shelter," he said. "Stand aside, and I'll show you." The people withdrew a little from Merlin and Vivien, and Merlin began a powerful conjuration. The earth trembled, and red dust rose into the air. Various forms appeared within this dust. A great structure took shape. The dust slowly cleared, revealing a magnificent castle. Its walls were red and ultramarine and adorned with gold statues.

Vivien kneeled before Merlin and kissed his hand. "This is wonderful. Will you teach me how to create a castle out of air?"

"I'll teach you that and more. I'll teach you how to make a castle vanish with a single touch of your wand and how to give something an entirely different appearance. I'll teach you many spells and charms."

"You're the most wonderful man in the world!" Vivien cried.

Merlin looked at her face, very beautiful in the moonlight, and felt intense love for her. "Do you still dislike me, Vivien?"

"Of course I don't dislike you!" she exclaimed. In truth she still hated Merlin.

Merlin and Vivien lived in the castle for more

than a year, during which he taught her all the magic that he could impart. Then Merlin said, "Vivien, you now have great powers of sorcery. There's nothing more for me to teach you."

Vivien rejoiced, thinking, "Now I'm going to bring about your death."

The next day Vivien had a great feast prepared. Using magic that Merlin had taught her, she created a strong sleeping potion that she put into a gold chalice of wine. At the end of the feast Vivien kneeled before Merlin and offered him the chalice. "I offer you this precious wine in a priceless chalice because your wisdom is precious and your life is priceless." She set her lips to the chalice but didn't drink; the wine merely touched her lips.

Suspecting no evil, Merlin took the chalice and cheerfully drank the wine. His vision soon clouded. "You've betrayed me!" he cried. He struggled to rise but couldn't.

Vivien sat with her chin on her hand, watching and smiling. Merlin sank into a deep sleep. Vivien leaned over him. With her forefinger she wove an invisible web of enchantment around him. When Merlin awoke, he couldn't move, not so much as a fingertip. He was like an insect enmeshed in the web of a cunning, beautiful spider. Vivien sat watching him. She laughed and said, "You're completely in my power, Merlin. You're trapped by a spell that you yourself taught me. You can't move at all without my permission.

Your life is over. Now *I'll* be the wisest and most powerful person in the world."

Merlin groaned. "I grieve at my folly, which has turned my own knowledge against me. Please grant me one favor."

"What is it?" Vivien asked.

"I perceive that King Arthur is in mortal danger. I beg you to use your powers to save him. If you do this good deed, you'll lessen the sin of your betrayal."

Having temporarily satisfied her desire to do evil, Vivian said, "Very well. What should I do?"

"Go into the west country, to the castle of Sir Domas de Noir. When you're there, you'll see how you can aid the king."

"This favor is the last one that anyone ever will do for you," Vivien said with satisfaction. She clapped her hands and summoned many of her servants. "Look how I've bewitched Merlin," she said. "Touch him. You'll see that he can't move." Servants touched Merlin's hands, arms, and face. Some even pulled his beard. He couldn't move, only groan. The servants laughed at him. Vivien magically created a large stone coffin and directed her servants to put Merlin inside it. She then had the coffin covered with a huge stone slab that ten men hardly could lift. Merlin lay, alive but helpless, inside the covered coffin.

Vivien made the magic castle vanish, replacing it with a mist that no one could penetrate.

Then she and her court left the valley. Vivien rejoiced that she had triumphed over Merlin, whom she left to die inside the coffin. However, as she had promised, she went to the castle of Domas de Noir.

Chapter 15

Morgan le Fay returned to Camelot. Feigning humility, she kneeled before Arthur, bowing her face. "Brother, I was wrong to speak against you and rebel against your royal authority. I beg your forgiveness."

Much moved, Arthur took Morgan's hand, lifted her to her feet, and kissed her brow and eyes. "Sister, I feel no ill will toward you. My heart holds nothing but love for you." So Morgan lived at Arthur's court as before, with Arthur believing that they were reconciled.

One day Morgan asked Arthur to show her Excalibur. Arthur took her by the hand and led her to the room with the strong wooden box containing the sword. Arthur opened the box, and Morgan saw Excalibur in its sheath. "Take this sword and examine it as you please," Arthur said.

Morgan removed Excalibur and drew it from its sheath. The sword flashed like lightning. "This is a very beautiful sword," she said. "May I continue to enjoy it by keeping it for a while?"

Eager to remain reconciled with his half sister, Arthur said, "Keep it as long as you like."

Morgan took Excalibur to her chamber and hid it under her mattress. Then she summoned eight goldsmiths, eight armor smiths, and eight jewelers. Showing them Excalibur, she said, "Make me a sword exactly like this one." The craftsmen labored with great diligence for two weeks and made a copy of Excalibur. Morgan then kept both swords.

Arthur proclaimed a hunt for his entire court. The day before the hunt Morgan said to him, "Brother, to show my love I want to give you a beautiful, noble horse." She called, and two grooms brought a black horse with silver trappings.

Neither Arthur nor anyone with him had ever seen such a beautiful horse. Delighted, he said, "This is the best gift I've received in a long time."

"It's a token of reconciliation," Morgan said. "Please ride him in the hunt tomorrow."

"I will," Arthur said.

In the afternoon, the hounds found the trail of a magnificent buck. Arthur and his court eagerly chased the buck. Arthur's new horse easily outran all the other horses except the one belonging to Sir Accolon of Gaul. Arthur and Accolon raced through the forest. They overtook the buck and cornered him in a thicket. Arthur killed him.

Arthur and Accolon now realized that they

were lost. They wandered until evening, when they felt hungry and weary. "It seems we'll have to sleep under a tree tonight," Arthur said.

"Maybe we should let our horses find their way through this wilderness," Accolon said. "Their instinct may lead them to some habitation."

Arthur agreed. He let his horse's bridle rein go loose, and the horse proceeded down a path. Accolon's horse followed. Before it was entirely dark, Arthur and Accolon emerged from the forest. Before them was a wide estuary with a beach of smooth white sand. Arthur and Accolon stood on the shore, seeing no habitation. A ship rapidly sailed toward them from the distance and halted nearby. It was painted many colors and had silk sails woven in various colors and embroidered with figures. "Let's look at this ship," Arthur said. "I've never seen one like it. It might be a fairy ship."

Arthur and Accolon rode up to the ship. Curtains at its far end parted, and twelve beautiful women came forward. Each wore a garment of scarlet satin, gold bracelets, and a gold head circlet. "Welcome, King Arthur. Welcome, Sir Accolon," they said.

"Fair ladies, how do you know our names?" Arthur asked. "Who are you?"

"We know all about you. We're part fairy," one lady said. "Please come aboard and eat, drink, and rest."

Arthur and Accolon accepted the invitation. A gangplank was dropped, and they rode up it. As soon as they were onboard, the ship swiftly sailed away. The ladies helped Arthur and Accolon dismount, took their horses away, and led them to a beautiful chamber at the ship's far end. The chamber contained a table spread with a linen cloth and set with savory meats, loaves of white bread, and excellent wines. Arthur and Accolon sat down and eagerly ate and drank. The ladies served them, conversed with them, and played lutes and citterns. Arthur and Accolon were content.

After a while Arthur felt very sleepy. "Fair ladies," he said, "you've greatly refreshed and entertained us. Do you have a place for us to sleep?"

"Lord, this boat has been prepared for you," one lady said. Arthur and Accolon were each led to a beautiful bedroom. Arthur lay down and immediately fell into a deep sleep.

When Arthur awoke, he found himself on a pallet in a dungeon. He bolted upright. All around him were captive knights, strangers to him. They numbered twenty-two. "Sirs, who are you? Where are we?"

One knight answered, "We're prisoners in the castle of Sir Domas le Noir."

"Do any of you know how I got here or what has become of my companion?" Arthur asked.

The same knight responded, "Last night two men dressed in black brought you here. You were asleep. They put you on that pallet. We haven't seen your companion."

"I've never heard of Sir Domas before. Who is he?" Arthur asked.

The knight answered, "Domas is a false knight, a treacherous coward. But he's powerful, of great estate, and cunning. Domas has a younger brother named Ontzlake. When their father died, each brother was to receive half of the family property. But Domas has taken nearly all of the estates. Sir Ontzlake has only one castle and its adjacent lands, which he keeps through force of arms and his own courage. Domas is so greedy that he wants even the one castle and small estate that his brother currently holds. But he's too cowardly to fight his brother himself, so for a long time he's been looking for a knight who will fight Sir Ontzlake in his behalf. For this reason he captures knights and gives them a choice between fighting Sir Ontzlake or languishing in prison. All of us here have refused to fight in Domas's behalf because he's so evil."

"Well," Arthur said, "I'd rather fight than be a prisoner for the rest of my life. If I fight Sir Ontzlake and win, I'll then deal with Sir Domas in a way he won't like."

Soon after, a guard opened the dungeon door. A young woman entered and went up to

Arthur. "Sir," she said, "I'm sorry to see such a noble-looking knight in this sad situation. If you'll serve this castle's lord, Sir Domas, by fighting his enemy Sir Ontzlake, you'll be free to go."

"Lady," Arthur replied, "I'll fight under one condition: if I win, all of these men must also go free."

"Very well," the woman said.

Arthur looked at her more closely. "I think I've seen you before."

"That's hardly possible because I'm Sir Domas's daughter," she lied. In truth she was a lady of Morgan le Fay and one of the women who had beguiled Arthur onto the ship. As commanded by Morgan, she had brought Arthur to the castle and delivered him into Domas's hands.

"Before I do battle for Sir Domas, you must deliver a sealed letter from me to Queen Morgan le Fay at King Arthur's court," Arthur said.

"Very well," the woman said.

Arthur wrote to Morgan that she should send him Excalibur. When Morgan received the message, she laughed and sent Arthur the sword made to look like Excalibur.

Domas informed his brother that he now had a champion who would do battle in his behalf. The news greatly troubled Sir Ontzlake because he was bedridden with severe wounds; in a recent tournament a spear had been thrust through both his thighs.

Chapter 16

When Accolon awoke, he found himself beside a marble fountain. Nearby a large pavilion of brightly-colored silk stood at the edge of a fair meadow. Accolon was astonished to find himself here instead of on the ship where he had fallen asleep. Feeling afraid, he thought, "The fairies on that ship have used magic to separate King Arthur and me." He crossed himself and prayed, "God save King Arthur from any harm." As Accolon rose, a dwarf came out of the pavilion. The dwarf greeted Accolon in a friendly, respectful way.

"Who are you?" Accolon asked.

"Sir, I serve Lady Gomyne, the lady of this pavilion. She has sent me to invite you in for refreshments."

"How did I get here?" Accolon said.

"I don't know. When we looked out this morning, we saw you lying by the fountain."

After washing at the fountain, Accolon accompanied the dwarf into the pavilion. In the center of it was a silver table spread with a white cloth covered with food. The curtains on the pavilion's far side parted, and Lady Gomyne entered from another room. She welcomed Accolon, who said, "Lady Gomyne, you're very kind to invite me in."

"It's a pleasure to have the company of such a worthy knight," Gomyne said. "Will you join me for breakfast?"

Accolon happily agreed because he was hungry and thirsty and Gomyne was beautiful. Accolon and Gomyne sat, and the dwarf waited on them. "Sir Knight, you look very strong," Gomyne said.

"It isn't seemly for me to praise myself, but it's true that I've engaged in several battles, and my friends and enemies consider me an able warrior," Accolon said.

"I know a worthy knight in sad need of such service as you might render."

"What is that service?" Accolon asked.

"Sir Ontzlake lives nearby. He has an older brother named Domas. Sir Domas has deprived Sir Ontzlake of nearly all his rightful inheritance, so Sir Ontzlake has very little of the property that belonged to their father. Sir Domas begrudges Sir Ontzlake even the little that he has, so Sir Ontzlake has to defend his one castle through force of arms. Sir Domas has found a champion of great strength and courage who is willing to

fight Sir Ontzlake in Sir Domas's behalf. Sir Ontzlake is unfit to fight because he recently was severely wounded in a tournament. I think that a knight could have no better reason to show his prowess than Sir Ontzlake's defense."

"Lady, I'd happily assist Sir Ontzlake except that I have no armor or weapons."

Gomyne smiled and said, "I'm sure Sir Ontzlake will provide you with suitable armor. As for a weapon, I have a sword that has no equal but one." She went to the curtained room from which she had come and soon returned with something wrapped in scarlet cloth. She opened the cloth and revealed Excalibur. "This sword will be yours if you'll fight in Sir Ontzlake's behalf."

Amazed, Accolon thought, "This sword is either Excalibur or its twin." He drew the blade from its sheath, and it shone with extraordinary splendor. Accolon said, "This sword is indeed the very image of another. I'd be willing to fight any battle to win this sword."

On the appointed day, Domas and Ontzlake came to the field of battle with their champions and attendants. Ontzlake was brought on a litter because of his wounds. Many people came to watch the combat, news of which had spread a considerable distance. Arthur and Accolon were fully armed and mounted. Their closed helmets concealed their faces. The herald came forward and announced that the battle was about to begin. Arthur and Accolon readied themselves. When the word was given, they rushed forward and collided with a thunderous roar. Their spears shattered. Each knight jumped from his horse with great skill, threw aside the remnant of his spear, and drew his sword.

Arthur and Accolon repeatedly struck at each other. Arthur's sword failed to penetrate Accolon's armor, but Excalibur deeply penetrated Arthur's. This happened again and again. Accolon didn't bleed at all, but Arthur's armor soon was stained with blood that flowed from many wounds. The grass all around Arthur was red with his blood. He began to fear that he would die. "Has Excalibur lost its power?" he wondered. "If I didn't know otherwise, I'd think that my enemy's sword—not mine—is Excalibur." In desperation Arthur struck Accolon so heavily on his helmet that Accolon almost fell to the ground. But with that blow Arthur's sword broke at the handle. The blade fell into the grass, leaving Arthur holding only the hilt.

Accolon ran at Arthur, intending to deal him a heavy blow. But when he saw that Arthur was weaponless, he paused. "Sir Knight," Accolon said, "I see that you have no weapon and have lost a great deal of blood. If you'll yield to me, I'll spare your life."

Although afraid to die, Arthur felt that he couldn't yield because he was the king. "Sir Knight, I can't yield to you. To do so would cost me my honor. I'd rather die. If you slay me while I'm weaponless, that will dishonor you, not me."

"I won't spare you unless you yield," Accolon said.

"I won't yield," Arthur replied.

"Then, stand back so that I can strike you." Arthur stood back, and Accolon struck him a blow that made him drop to his knees. Accolon raised Excalibur to strike Arthur again. Most of the spectators cried out to Accolon to spare the life of such a brave knight, but Accolon wouldn't.

Having come to Domas's castle as she had promised Merlin, Vivien was among the spectators. She realized that the brave knight must be King Arthur. She now fulfilled her promise to aid him. Clapping her hands together, Vivien cast a spell that made Accolon feel as if he had received a powerful blow to his arm. His hand and arm went numb, and Excalibur fell from his grasp onto the grass. Arthur now recognized Accolon's sword as Excalibur and knew that he'd been betrayed. "Treason!" he cried. "Treason!" Before Accolon could stop him, Arthur seized Excalibur. Feeling an infusion of strength, Arthur rose, ran at Accolon, and struck him so forcefully that Excalibur penetrated Accolon's armor. Arthur struck Accolon again and again. Accolon cried out and fell onto his hands and knees. Arthur grabbed Excalibur's sheath from Accolon and flung it away. Accolon's wounds then spurted blood. Arthur yanked off Accolon's helmet with the aim of slaying him. Blinded by his own blood, Arthur still didn't recognize Accolon, so he said, "Sir Knight, who are you? I want to know who has betrayed me."

"I haven't betrayed anyone," Accolon answered. "I'm Sir Accolon of Gaul, a knight of King Arthur's court."

Taking off his helmet, Arthur yelled, "I'm your master—King Arthur!"

Accolon fainted from shock and blood loss. Then Arthur also fainted. Spectators rushed over the barriers to aid the two knights. Many wailed. Vivien came out onto the field and said of Arthur, "I can cure his wounds." She commanded that two stretchers be brought. Arthur was placed on one and Accolon on the other. Vivian had them both taken to a nearby nunnery. In the nunnery Vivien examined Arthur's wounds and bathed them with balsam. They immediately began to heal. A servant washed and dressed Accolon's wounds but didn't apply the balsam.

The next morning Arthur was weak and sick but able to rise. He got up from his couch, wrapped a cloak around him, and went to the place where Accolon lay. He questioned Accolon, who told Arthur everything that had happened to him. Arthur said, "You're blameless in this matter. I fear that there's treachery here aimed at my downfall." Arthur found Vivien and said, "Lady, please dress Sir Accolon's wounds with the same balsam that you applied to mine."

"Lord, I don't have any more of that balsam," she said, but she was lying. That afternoon Accolon died of his wounds.

Arthur summoned Domas and Ontzlake into his presence. They kneeled before him in fear of his majesty. Arthur said, "Sir Domas, because you're false and treasonable, I hereby give all of your possessions to Sir Ontzlake and give you the one castle currently in his possession. Further, I forbid you to ride any horse other than a lady's horse; you aren't worthy to ride a warhorse, as a true knight is. I also command you to free all the knights you've imprisoned and compensate them for the injury you've done them in a way determined by a court of chivalry." Arthur then dismissed both Domas and Ontzlake.

Chapter 17

On a pleasant spring day Guinevere went on an outing with some ladies and knights of her court. The sunlight was golden and the breeze gentle. The birds sang. Flowers of many different kinds bloomed all around, carpeting entire meadows. Guinevere and her court walked among the blossoms.

A young woman dressed in sky blue came riding across the meadow on a white horse, accompanied by three pages also dressed in sky blue. The woman wore a gold chain around her neck and a gold circlet on her head. Her hair was blond and adorned with blue ribbons embroidered with gold. One of the pages carried a small square frame wrapped in crimson satin.

Guinevere directed Pellias to go meet the young woman. When Pellias reached her, he said, "Fair lady, Queen Guinevere has directed me to greet you and ask your name and purpose."

"Sir Knight, I see from your bearing and way of speaking that you're a lord of high estate and great nobility. My name is Parcenet. I belong to the court of Lady Ettard of Grantmesnle, which is a considerable distance from here. I've come to see Queen Guinevere."

Pellias led Parcenet to Guinevere, who received Parcenet graciously and asked, "What is it that you desire?"

"The people of my region consider my mistress, Lady Ettard of Grantmesnle, the most beautiful woman in the world. Having recently heard of your great beauty, she sent me to see with my own eyes if the reports were true. Now that I stand before you, I have to say that you're the most beautiful lady I've ever seen, with the possible exception of Lady Ettard."

Guinevere laughed merrily. "I find it amusing that you've traveled so far about such a trivial matter. Tell me: what is your page carrying so carefully?"

"It's a portrait of my mistress."

"Show it to me," Guinevere said.

The page dismounted, kneeled before Guinevere, and uncovered the picture. It was beautifully painted on an ivory panel framed with gold inset with jewels. The lady depicted was extraordinarily beautiful. "Your mistress is indeed graced with wondrous beauty," Guinevere said. "If she's as beautiful as her picture indicates, I think she must be the most beautiful woman in the world."

Pellias looked at the picture and said, "Lady, I protest. You're more beautiful."

"Sir Knight," Parcenet said, "it's a good thing you say those words so far from Grantmesnle, where Sir Engamore of Malverat, a very strong knight, maintains that Lady Ettard is the world's most beautiful woman and challenges anyone who says otherwise to fight him."

Pellias kneeled before Guinevere and set his palms together. "Lady, please do me the honor of accepting me as your champion in this matter. If you grant me leave, I'll go meet this knight and throw him in your honor."

Guinevere laughed. "I'm greatly pleased that you would fight for me over such a small matter. That means that you certainly would fight for me in a serious situation. I happily accept you as my champion in this affair. Go arm yourself."

"With your permission I'll go as I am. I believe I can win armor and weapons along the way, in which case this adventure will do you even more credit."

"As you wish," Guinevere said, pleased. She ordered her page to fetch the best horse that he could obtain for Pellias. The page ran off and quickly returned with a completely black horse. Pellias said goodbye to the queen and her court. Everyone praised him and wished him well. He rode away with Parcenet and her three pages.

After some distance Parcenet said, "Sir, I

don't know your name."

"I'm Pellias, a knight of King Arthur's Round Table."

Parcenet was astonished because many people considered Pellias the best fighter alive except for Arthur and Pellinore. "It certainly will be a great honor for Sir Engamore to fight a knight as famous as you."

"I think that several knights of the Round Table are better fighters than I am."

"I find that hard to believe." After a pause Parcenet asked, "How will you obtain armor?"

"I don't know yet. I have faith that I'll find appropriate armor before I battle Sir Engamore."

"It must be rare for a lady to have a knight as fine as you battle in her behalf."

"When your time comes, I hope you'll have a better knight to serve you."

"Not likely!" Parcenet exclaimed. Pellias laughed. "I wish I had a good knight to serve me," Parcenet said.

"I'll give you the first knight whom I defeat," Pellias said earnestly. Then he joked, "Would you like your knight to be short or tall? Fair or dark? If you prefer short and fair, I'll let any tall, dark ones go."

Parcenet looked steadily at Pellias. "I'd like him to be your height, have hair and eyes the same color as yours, have a straight nose like yours, and be as witty as you."

"Oh! I wish you'd told me this before we came so far from Camelot. I could easily have gotten you a knight there. Camelot has knights in such abundance that we keep them in wicker cages and sell them two for a farthing."

Parcenet laughed. "Then, Camelot must be a wonderful place."

Parcenet and Pellias continued to make merry conversation. They took much pleasure in the spring weather and lovely meadows. That night they stayed at a pleasant inn on the outskirts of the forest.

The next day they left early in the morning and entered the forest. After they had traveled a considerable distance, Parcenet said, "Do you know what part of the forest this is?"

"No," Pellias answered.

"It's sometimes called the Forest of Adventure. It's a place full of magic. People say that no knight can enter it without meeting with adventure."

"I'm glad to hear that," Pellias said. "Maybe I can obtain armor here."

They traveled a long way within the Forest of Adventure, which was dark and silent. When they emerged into an extensive opening, they saw a turbulent river in front of them. A woman withered with age sat under a thorn tree on the river's bank. Her eyes were red and watery. Many bristles grew on her cheeks and chin. No part of her face was free of wrinkles. As Pellias, Parcenet, and the three pages approached, the woman cried, "Sir, will you carry me over this river on your horse? I'm old and feeble and can't cross it on my own."

Parcenet rebuked the woman. "Be silent! Who are you to ask this noble knight to do you such a service?"

Pellias was displeased with Parcenet. "Lady," he said to her, "you speak improperly. A true knight gives aid to anyone who needs it. King Arthur is the model of knighthood, and he has taught us that." Pellias dismounted and lifted the old woman up onto his saddle. Then he remounted and rode into the river's ford, bringing the woman safely to the other side of the torrent. Parcenet and the three pages followed, marveling at Pellias' knightliness.

On the other shore Pellias dismounted, intending to help the old woman dismount. But she immediately leaped down lightly. The old woman had turned into a lady of extraordinary beauty. Her face was like smooth ivory. Her eyes were black and bright, like two jewels. She was dressed in green from head to foot. Her hair was long, black, and as soft and glossy as silk. She wore a gold necklace and gold bracelets, all of them set with opals and emeralds. Pellias marveled at the transformation and realized that she must be a fairy. He kneeled before her and set his hands together, palm to palm.

"Sir, why do you kneel to me?" the lady said.

"Because you're so wonderfully strange and beautiful."

"Arise. You've done me a good service. You're certainly an excellent knight."

Pellias stood. "Who are you?"

"I'm Nymue, the Lady of the Lake. I assumed the appearance of a feeble old woman to test your knightliness, and I've found you worthy." Smiling, Nymue removed her necklace and put it on Pellias. "Keep this," she said. "It has magical powers." And she vanished.

Half dazed, Pellias silently mounted his horse and rode on. The others followed, also silent. After some distance Parcenet said, "How wonderful!"

"Yes," Pellias said. Unknown to him, the necklace had the power to make people love its wearer.

Chapter 18

ater in the afternoon Pellias, Parcenet, and their attendants stopped in the forest to rest, eat, and drink. As they were refreshing themselves, they heard a loud lament. A lady rode out of the thickets on a spotted horse. A young squire dressed in green and white and seated on a reddish brown horse rode behind her. The lady's face was swollen from weeping. With no net or band to hold it in place, her hair hung down onto her shoulders. Her dress was torn by brambles and stained with forest travel. The squire, too, looked disheveled and distressed.

Pellias immediately went to the lady and stopped her horse by taking him by the bridle. "Lady, what troubles you so greatly?"

"Sir, it doesn't matter because you can't help me," she answered.

"Maybe I can," Pellias said. "I'd certainly like to."

"Your intentions are kind," the lady said, observing Pellias more closely. "If you were in armor and had a weapon, you might have helped me, but I see that you're in holiday attire."

"I might be able to help you if you'll tell me what's wrong." Still holding her horse by the bridle, Pellias brought the lady to the place where Parcenet and the others were picnicking. Pellias gently persuaded the lady to dismount, sit, and eat and drink.

When she had eaten and drunk some wine, the lady felt somewhat better. "Sir Knight," she said, "I'm Lady Alice. I live a considerable distance from here. A month ago I happily married Sir Brandemere. Today at dawn he and I set out for a hunt, with our squire Ponteferet and a hound my husband loves. Within the forest a doe started up. The hound immediately pursued her. I, my husband, and Ponteferet followed with great spirit. After chasing the doe a great distance, we came to a violent river crossed by a long, narrow stone bridge. On the other side of the river was a castle with seven towers. The castle seemed to emerge from the rocks on which it was built. As we approached the bridge, the castle's gate was raised and the drawbridge was dropped with a bang. A knight dressed entirely in red thundered out of the castle. His spear and all of his horse's trappings also were red. He stopped at the other end of the bridge and yelled at my husband, 'Where are you going, Sir Knight?' Sir Brandemere replied, 'Sir, I wish to cross this bridge because my hound, whom I love, has crossed here in pursuit of a doe.' The Red Knight bellowed, 'If you come onto this bridge, you do so at your peril. This bridge belongs to me. No one can cross it without first throwing me.' My husband was dressed only in light outdoor clothing. His helmet was too light for battle. However, he wouldn't tolerate the Red Knight's effrontery. Telling Ponteferet and me to remain where we were, he drew his sword and rode to the middle of the bridge. Dressed in full armor, the Red Knight threw aside his spear, drew his sword, and rode forward to meet my husband. He lifted himself in his stirrups and struck my husband on the head with his sword. The blade cut through my husband's helmet and into his head. Blood poured down into my husband's face. He fell from his horse and lay as if dead. The Red Knight dismounted and laid my husband across the saddle of my husband's horse. Then he took both horses by the bridle and led them across the bridge and into his castle. The gate immediately closed behind him, and the drawbridge was raised. The Red Knight paid no attention to Ponteferet or me. He left without saying anything. I don't know what has happened to my husband or even whether he's alive." Tears streamed down Alice's face.

Greatly moved, Pellias said, "Lady Alice, I grieve for you and want to help you. Lead me to

PATRON CHARGED ITEMS

PTN: 809242247
GRP: STUDENT

Due:	Title/Item Barcode
5/9/2016 08:00 PM	King Arthur and his knigh 0072638Q 428.64 PYLE-H 2007k 1

the Red Knight's castle. I'll do my utmost to find out what has happened to your husband."

"I'm grateful for your goodwill, but you can't hope to succeed at so dangerous an undertaking without armor and weapons. Consider how the Red Knight has treated my husband, who had no armor. It isn't likely he'll show you more consideration."

Parcenet and Ponteferet urged Pellias not to confront the Red Knight without armor and weapons. "Don't attempt to stop me," Pellias responded. "I've undertaken more dangerous tasks several times and escaped without serious injury." Pellias helped Alice and Parcenet mount their horses. Then he, Ponteferet, and the other men mounted their horses, and the entire group left for the Red Knight's castle.

After journeying a great distance through the forest, they came to a steep, bare hill. At the top they saw beneath them a turbulent river spanned by a narrow bridge. On the far side of the bridge was a high castle with seven towers. Ponteferet pointed. "Sir Knight, that's the Red Knight's castle."

"Lady Alice," Pellias said, "I'll inquire about your husband." He galloped down the hill. When Pellias was near the bridge, the castle's gate was raised and the drawbridge fell with a bang. The Red Knight rode quickly and threateningly toward the bridge. Pellias turned to his companions, who had followed him down the hill, "Stay where you are. I'll go forward to speak to this knight."

"Don't go, Sir Knight," Ponteferet said. "You'll be hurt."

"I won't be hurt," Pellias said, and he ventured onto the bridge.

"Who dares come onto this bridge?" the Red Knight yelled.

"Discourteous knight, I'm Sir Pellias. I've come to ask what you've done with Sir Brandemere and why you've treated him so grievously."

The Red Knight answered, "Surrender to me, and I'll bring you to him. Because you're unarmed, I don't want to fight you. However, if you don't immediately surrender, I'll *make* you surrender."

"What!" Pellias exclaimed. "You would attack an unarmed man?"

"If you don't immediately surrender," the Red Knight said.

"You aren't fit to be called a knight," Pellias said. "If I fight you, it will be to your disgrace." Pellias looked around for anything that he could use as a weapon. He saw a huge, loose stone in the top layer of one wall of the bridge. This stone was too heavy for five men of ordinary strength to lift. However, Pellias easily lifted it in both hands. He ran toward the Red Knight and flung the stone at him with great force. The stone hit the middle of the Red Knight's shield and drove it against his chest. The Red Knight fell backward to the ground with a loud clang and lay unconscious. Pellias ran to the Red Knight and pressed his knee into the Red Knight's chest. He unlaced the Red Knight's helmet and removed it, revealing a strong, handsome face. The Red Knight was regaining consciousness. Pellias pulled the Red Knight's dagger from its sheath and set the point to the Red Knight's throat.

The Red Knight pleaded, "Spare my life!"

"Who are you?" Pellias demanded.

"Sir Adresack of the Seven Towers."

"What have you done with Sir Brandemere? How is he?"

"He isn't as seriously wounded as you suppose," Adresack answered.

"Lady Alice," Pellias called, "your husband is alive!"

"Thank God!" Alice cried.

"Do you have other captives in your castle besides Sir Brandemere?" Pellias asked Adresack.

"There are twenty-one other captives: eighteen knights and squires and three ladies. I've defended this bridge for a long time. I've taken captive anyone who has tried to cross it and held them for ransom. As a result, I've accumulated great wealth."

"You're an evil man. I should kill you," Pellias said. "However, since you've asked for mercy, I'll grant it provided that you agree to two things. First, you must go to Queen Guinevere in Camelot and tell her that I've taken your armor and that I'll wear it when defending her honor. Second, you must confess all of your crimes to King Arthur and ask him to spare your life."

"I promise to do these things if you'll spare my life," Adresack said.

Pellias permitted him to rise. "Remove this knight's weapons and armor, and put the armor on me," Pellias said to Ponteferet, who did as directed. "Now," Pellias said to Adresack, "take me into your castle."

Inside the castle, Pellias ordered Adresack, "Lead me to the dungeon." There they found Brandemere and the other prisoners. Alice ran to her husband. They embraced and wept with joy. Two knights from Arthur's court were among the captives: Sir Brandiles and Sir Mador de la Porte. Upon seeing Pellias, Brandiles and Mador joyfully embraced him and kissed him on both cheeks. All of the freed captives rejoiced. They thanked and praised Pellias, who was very pleased. Pellias angrily turned to Adresack. "Go do as I've ordered you. If you don't leave right away, I may well decide to be less merciful."

Adresack immediately summoned his squire, and the two rode off to Camelot. Pellias and the freed captives went through Adresack's castle. They found four caskets of fine jewels and thirteen chests of gold and silver coins—all of which had been acquired as ransom. In recompense for their suffering Pellias gave a casket of jewels to Alice and each of the three ladies who had been held captive. He ordered that the money be equally divided among the male captives. "Sir Knight," one of the captives said to Pellias, "you should have a share of the treasure." All the others agreed.

"No," Pellias said. "You've suffered at Sir Adresack's hands and should be compensated. I haven't suffered." The others praised Pellias' generosity. All of the knights vowed to be faithful to him unto death.

When the treasure had been divided, Brandemere invited everyone to his castle for rest, refreshment, and entertainment. For three days there was great rejoicing, with feasting and jousting. On the fourth day Pellias, Parcenet, and the pages prepared to travel on, although the others begged Pellias to stay a while longer. Brandiles and Mador asked if they could accompany Pellias, who finally agreed.

Chapter 19

In the afternoon the travelers emerged from the forest. Farm fields, pastures, and plantations of trees with fragrant blossoms spread before them. "This is a beautiful place," Pellias said.

"I'm glad you like it because this is my home," Parcenet said. "All of this land belongs to Lady Ettard. From the top of that hill you'll be able to see the castle of Grantmesnle in the valley below."

"Let's go!" Pellias said. "I'm eager to see it." They galloped up the hill, from which they saw the beautiful castle, built entirely of red stone. A small town surrounded the castle. People came and went along its streets. "That's certainly an excellent estate," Pellias said.

"Those of us who live there think so," Parcenet said.

"That glade of young trees near the castle looks like a pleasant spot," Pellias said. "My companions and I will set up camp there. Meanwhile, please go to Lady Ettard and tell her that a knight has come who holds that Lady Guinevere of Camelot is the most beautiful woman in the world. Tell her that I'll defend that claim. If she has a champion who will fight in her behalf, I'll meet him in that field tomorrow at noon."

"Sir Pellias," Parcenet said, "I'll do as you wish. Although I don't want you to win the encounter, I hope you won't be injured. You're a valiant, gentle knight, and I feel friendship for you. I'm sorry to leave you."

Pellias laughed. "Parcenet, you praise me more than I deserve."

"No. You deserve anything that I can say to your credit." Parcenet and her pages went their way.

Pellias, Brandiles, and Mador set up three pavilions: one white, one red, and one green. Over the white pavilion Pellias hung his banner, which showed three swans on a white background. Brandiles hung his red banner over the red pavilion; it showed an armored hand holding a banner. Mador hung his green banner over the green pavilion; it showed a crow holding a white lily in one claw and a sword in the other.

Noon of the next day, Pellias went to the field in front of the castle. He was dressed from head to foot in the red armor that he'd taken from Adresack. Looking very fierce, he rode up and down in front of the castle walls, shouting, "I'm a knight of King Arthur's Round Table. I maintain that King Arthur's queen, Lady Guinevere of Camelot, is the most beautiful woman in the world. If any knight maintains otherwise, let him defend his opinion with his body."

Pellias caused a great commotion within the castle. Many people came to the walls and looked down at him. After some time the castle's drawbridge was lowered. Sir Engamore, a huge knight of proud demeanor, rode out. He wore green armor and green sleeves. Engamore approached Pellias, who rode forward to meet him. They courteously saluted each other. "Sir Knight, will you do me the favor of telling me your name?" Engamore asked.

"I'm Sir Pellias."

"Sir Pellias, it's a great honor for me to meet such a famous knight. Everyone in the courts of chivalry has heard of you. If I have the good fortune to throw you, all of your honor will become mine. I'm Sir Engamore of Malverat. I've defended Lady Ettard's claim to peerless beauty for eleven months against all challengers. If I successfully defend her claim one month longer, I'll become her husband and the lord of all this fair estate. I'll do my utmost to honor her."

"Sir Engamore, thank you for your courteous words. I, too, will do my utmost in this encounter."

Pellias and Engamore saluted each other with their spears and rode to their places. Many people had come down to the castle's lower walls to watch the friendly contest. A herald came from the castle and gave the signal to begin. Pellias and Engamore galloped toward each other with such speed that the ground shook. When they met, Engamore's spear burst into thirty pieces. Pellias' spear remained intact. Engamore was hurtled from his saddle onto the ground more than a spear's length behind his horse. The spectators on the walls cried out in dismay because Engamore was their greatest knight. Ettard cried out especially strongly because she loved Engamore and feared that he might have been killed.

Three squires ran to Engamore, lifted him up, and unlaced his helmet to give him air. He was alive but unconscious. Gradually he opened his eyes. Pellias was relieved because he would have been very sorry to have slain him. Engamore vehemently demanded that Pellias fight him on foot with swords. "No, Sir Engamore," Pellias said. "I won't engage in such a serious fight with you. I wish you no ill." Engamore wept with vexation and shame. Brandiles and Mador congratulated Pellias. They also tried to console Engamore, but he wouldn't be comforted.

Ettard emerged from the castle with many squires and ladies and crossed the meadow to Pellias and Engamore. At her approach Pellias drew his dagger, cut the straps of his helmet, and removed the helmet. He went forward, bare-headed, to meet Ettard. Pellias saw that she was much more beautiful than her portrait had indicated. He kneeled on the grass in front of Ettard, set his hands together palm to palm, and said, "Lady, I beg your forgiveness for doing battle against your credit. I did so to honor my queen. Excepting her, I'd rather be your champion than that of any other woman I've ever seen."

Pellias was wearing the necklace of gold, opals, and emeralds that Nymue had given him. Therefore, when Ettard looked at him, she fell in love with him. Ettard smiled at Pellias, gave him her hand, and bade him rise. "Sir Knight, you're a very famous warrior. Anyone who knows anything of chivalry has heard of Sir Pellias, the Gentle Knight. Although my champion Sir Engamore has defeated all challengers until now, he should feel no shame at having been defeated by such a strong knight."

Pellias was grateful for Ettard's gracious words. He introduced Brandiles and Mador, and Ettard invited the three knights into her castle for refreshments and entertainment. Pellias, Brandiles, and Mador returned to their pavilions and put on fine clothes and jewelry. Then they went to the castle. Everyone present thought they looked wonderfully noble.

Engamore had recovered from his fall, but he was downcast. He thought, "Who am I in the presence of these noble lords?"

Ettard gave a fine feast. Pellias sat to her right and Engamore to her left. Before, Engamore always had sat to Ettard's right. Ettard couldn't stop looking at Pellias. After the feast the two of them walked on the castle grounds. When it came time for Pellias to leave, Ettard asked him to stay. He happily agreed because he was very taken with Ettard's graciousness and beauty. Brandiles and Mador returned to their pavilions.

That evening Ettard and Pellias dined together. Parcenet waited on Ettard. Pages and squires played harps, and ladies of Ettard's court sang sweetly. Pellias felt as if he were in paradise. "Lady," he said to Ettard, "I'd like to do something to show how highly I regard and honor you."

Ettard had continually looked at Pellias's necklace, which she desired to have. She said, "You'd do me a great favor if you'd give me your beautiful necklace."

Pellias's face fell. "I can't do that. I obtained this necklace in an extraordinary way and can't part with it."

"Why not?"

Pellias told Ettard about Nymue.

"That's a wonderful story," Ettard said. "If you can't give me the necklace, will you at least let me wear it a little while? I'm greatly taken with its beauty. Please let me wear it."

Pellias felt he couldn't refuse. "Lady, you'll have it to wear for a while." He removed the necklace and hung it around Ettard's neck. Now that Pellias no longer wore the necklace, Ettard saw him differently. She thought, "What ailed me that I was so enchanted with Pellias, to the discredit of Engamore, who has served me so faithfully? Hasn't Pellias discredited me? Didn't he come here expressly for that purpose? Didn't he throw my true knight in scorn of me? What's wrong with me that I've bestowed such regard on him?" Without showing her changed feelings, Ettard began to consider how she might get revenge on Pellias. "He's my enemy," she thought, "and he's in my power." Making an excuse, Ettard left Pellias. She took Parcenet aside and said, "Fetch me a powerful sleeping draft."

"Lady, what are you planning to do?" Parcenet asked. "Are you going to give that noble knight a sleeping draft?"

"Yes."

"Lady, that surely would be wrong. He sits peacefully at your table as your guest."

"Do as I tell you," Ettard responded. Afraid to disobey, Parcenet brought the sleeping draft in a chalice of wine.

Ettard took the chalice to Pellias. "Sir Knight, drink this wine in the same measure in which you feel goodwill toward me."

Parcenet stood behind Ettard's chair. When Pellias took the chalice, Parcenet frowned and shook her head at him. But Pellias didn't notice. He was too focused on Ettard's beauty. "Lady," he said to Ettard, "if this wine contained poison, I'd still drink it if you asked me to." Pellias drank. Surprised, he said, "This wine is bitter." His head soon felt extremely heavy. Pellias slumped forward. His head drooped onto the table.

After a little while Ettard said, "Sir Knight, are you asleep?" Pellias didn't answer. The draft had put him to sleep. Laughing, Ettard clapped her hands to summon her servants. "Take this knight to an inner room," she ordered. "Strip him of everything but his undergarment. Then put him on a pallet and carry him to the place where he threw Sir Engamore. When morning comes, everyone will see him in his undergarment. He'll be humiliated in the very spot where he humiliated Sir Engamore." Parcenet was very distressed to hear this. She withdrew and wept for Pellias.

The next morning Pellias awoke with the sun shining into his face. At first he didn't know where he was. He sat up and saw that he lay beneath the castle walls near the back gate. Above him, atop the wall, were many people. When they saw that Pellias was awake, they mocked him and laughed. Ettard gazed down from a window. Pellias saw her laughing at him. He realized that he was dressed only in his undergarment. "This can't be happening. It must be a nightmare," he thought.

The back gate opened, and Parcenet came out. Her face was wet with tears. Holding a red cloak, she ran to Pellias. "Good and gentle knight, wrap this around you."

Pellias now knew that this was no dream. Trembling with shame, he wrapped the cloak around him. "Thank you, maiden."

The people on the walls hooted and reviled Parcenet. She ran back into the castle. Staggering with amazement and shame, Pellias went to his pavilion. Once inside he threw himself onto his couch. When Brandiles and Mador heard what had happened, they hurried to Pellias. They were enraged at what had been done to him. "We'll get help from Camelot," they said to Pellias. "We'll burst open Lady Ettard's castle and bring her here to beg your pardon for this affront. We'll get her here even if we have to drag her by her hair."

Pellias didn't lift his head. "No," he said. "You can't treat a woman that way. Even now I'd defend her honor unto death. I must be bewitched because I love her passionately."

Brandiles and Mador were astounded. "Lady Ettard has laid some powerful spell on him," Brandiles said to Mador, who agreed. Pellias asked them to leave. They left feeling angry with him.

Pellias continued to lie on his couch until the afternoon. Then he roused himself and put on his armor. When Brandiles and Mador saw Pellias in his armor, they hurried over to him. "What are you going to do?" Brandiles asked.

"I'm going to try to speak with Lady Ettard," Pellias answered.

"Have you gone crazy?" Mador exclaimed.

"I don't know," Pellias said. "I think that if I don't see Lady Ettard and talk to her, I'll die of longing."

"This is madness!" Brandiles said.

"I don't know whether it's madness or some enchantment," Pellias said. He armed from head to foot, mounted his horse, and rode to the castle.

When Ettard saw Pellias again parading in front of the castle, she called six of her best knights to her. "Sirs, there's that knight who brought so much shame on us yesterday. Punish him as he deserves."

The six knights armed themselves and rode out toward Pellias. When Pellias saw them, he felt enraged and rode against them. At first they withstood him, but he fought with fury, so they soon fled. Pellias pursued them around the field and knocked four of them from their horses. Then suddenly he stopped fighting and said to the remaining two knights, "I surrender."

The two knights, who had greatly feared

Pellias, were astonished. They laid hands on him and took him toward the castle. Pellias thought, "Now I'll get to speak to Lady Ettard." But he was mistaken. When Pellias was about to enter the castle, Ettard called down from a window to her two knights, "What are you doing?"

"We're bringing him to you, Lady."

"No!" Ettard said vehemently. "Tie his hands behind his back, tie his feet under his horse's belly, and send him back to his companions."

Pellias looked up at Ettard and cried, "Lady, I surrendered to *you*, not to these unworthy knights."

"Drive him away!" Ettard demanded. "I hate the sight of him." The two knights bound Pellias to his horse, who bore him back to the pavilions.

When Brandiles and Mador saw Pellias's new humiliation, they felt intense grief and shame. They untied Pellias, and Brandiles cried, "Aren't you ashamed to permit this infamy?"

Trembling, Pellias said, "I don't care what happens to me."

"If you don't care about your own reputation," Mador said, "you still should care whether you bring shame on King Arthur and the Round Table!"

Pellias yelled, "I don't care about them either!" Brandiles and Mador were horrified.

Chapter 20

Queen Guinevere strongly disliked Sir Gawain. Stubborn, stern, and haughty, Gawain wouldn't follow Guinevere's commands as other knights of the royal court did. Also, Guinevere couldn't forget that Gawain had spoken to her disrespectfully and had refused to aid her when Cameliard was threatened.

Several days before Pellias's humiliation at Ettard's hands, Gawain, Griflet, and Sir Constantine of Cornwall were sitting with five ladies of Guinevere's court in a garden beneath Guinevere's tower. Guinevere sat at an open window, not far from the ground, that overlooked the garden. Unknown to them, Guinevere could overhear the ladies and knights. Gawain played the lute and sang a ballad so beautifully that Guinevere enjoyed listening to him.

Guinevere had a greyhound whom she loved. His collar was gold inset with garnets. The greyhound now came running into the garden. His feet were muddy. He ran up to Gawain and put his front paws on him in a friendly way. Dressed in sky-blue silk embroidered with silver, Gawain was angry that his clothes had been dirtied. He punched the greyhound in the head. The dog cried out. Guinevere angrily called from her window, "Why have you struck my dog, Sir?" The knights and ladies were startled to find that Guinevere had been watching and listening.

Gawain defiantly answered, "Your dog affronted me, Lady."

Furious, Guinevere said, "Your speech is overly bold, Sir."

"No, Lady. My speech is only bold enough to assert my rights."

Guinevere's face flamed, and her eyes flashed. "You forget to whom you speak."

Gawain smiled bitterly. "And you forget that I'm the son of a king so powerful that he needs no help from any other king to maintain his position."

Appalled by Gawain's boldness, his companions looked down at the ground. In a voice half smothered by anger, Guinevere said, "Sir Gawain, you're arrogant beyond measure. I've never heard anyone else reply to their queen as you've replied to me. This is my court. In it I command. I order you to leave and never return to any place where I hold my court. You deeply offend me. Don't show your face again unless you're prepared to ask for my forgiveness."

Gawain rose, bowed to Guinevere, and said,

"I'm going. I won't return until you're willing to apologize for the discourteous way you've treated me today and at other times in front of my peers." He left without looking behind him. Guinevere went to her chamber and wept with anger.

When Ewaine heard about the quarrel, he went straight to Gawain and asked what had happened. Upset, Gawain told Ewaine everything. Ewaine said, "You were wrong to speak to the queen that way. Nevertheless, if you're banished, I'll go with you because you're my cousin and dear companion." Ewaine went to King Arthur and said, "Lord, the queen has banished Sir Gawain. Although I can't say that he doesn't deserve this punishment, I ask your permission to go with him."

Arthur was very grieved, but he maintained a steadfast expression and said, "Sir, you're free to go where you please. As for your cousin—he was so offensive to the queen that she couldn't do otherwise than she did."

Accompanied by their squires, Ewaine and Gawain left Camelot. They traveled through the forest until twilight. Wondering where they would find shelter for the night, they came to the top of a hill from which they saw a lovely valley filled with cottages and well-kept farms. In the middle of the valley was a beautiful abbey. Gawain said to Ewaine, "If that's an abbey of monks, we should find excellent lodging there."

The abbey was indeed an abbey of monks.

Because Gawain and Ewaine were nobles, the abbot himself welcomed them and brought them into his own part of the abbey, where they were given an excellent supper. A merry man who delighted in company, the abbot asked Gawain and Ewaine why they were traveling. They said only that they were seeking adventure. "You can find adventure not far from here," the abbot said. "If you travel east, you'll come to a beautiful castle of gray stone. In front of the castle is a broad, level meadow. In the middle of the meadow is a sycamore tree. Upon the tree is a shield that some ladies repeatedly deface. If you forbid the ladies from defacing the shield, you'll have a good adventure."

Gawain said, "That's quite strange. We'll go there tomorrow." The abbot laughed merrily.

The next morning Gawain and Ewaine said goodbye to the abbot and rode east with their squires. After several hours they saw the gray castle. Its glass windows shown brightly in the summer sunlight. Gawain and Ewaine also saw the sycamore tree with the shield, which was black with three white hawks. Seven young women stood in front of the shield and defaced it. Some struck it with wooden rods. Others flung lumps of clay at it. A noble-looking knight in black armor but with no shield sat nearby on a black horse. The defaced shield clearly belonged to him, yet he in no way protested its treatment.

"How strange!" Ewaine said to Gawain. "I think I'll challenge that knight."

"I'm the older, more experienced knight," Gawain said. "*I'll* challenge him."

"Very well," Ewaine said. "You *are* much stronger than I am."

Gawain galloped to the sycamore tree. Holding his spear, he shouted, "Stop that!" The young women fled, shrieking.

The knight in black rode up to Gawain in a stately way and said, "Sir Knight, why have you interfered with those ladies?"

"They were dishonoring a knight's shield."

The Black Knight haughtily said, "That shield belongs to me. I'm capable of protecting it."

"It appears otherwise," Gawain said.

"Since you think you're better able to protect my shield than I am, you'll have to make good on your claim by fighting me."

Gawain readily agreed. The Black Knight took down his shield, put it on his arm, and took his spear in hand. Gawain also prepared for combat. Each knight went to his place. Forty or more ladies, squires, and others crowded onto the castle walls and looked down to see the combat. At Ewaine's signal each combatant shouted and galloped forward. Having never lost a fight except to King Arthur, Gawain was confident that he'd throw his opponent. However, his spear shattered whereas the Black Knight's spear remained intact. Thrown from his saddle, Gawain crashed into the dust. The people on the castle wall cheered. Gawain lay stunned with the blow and with astonishment. Then he got up. Enraged, he drew his sword and rushed at the Black Knight, who jumped from his saddle and drew his sword. A fierce swordfight followed. Ewaine galloped up and cried, "Sir Knights, there's no cause for such desperate battle!"

Gawain cried furiously at Ewaine, "Stand aside!"

"I'll fight him on horse or foot!" the Black Knight said of Gawain.

"Stop fighting!" Ewaine insisted. "For shame, Gawain! For shame to seek such desperate quarrel with a knight who met you in a friendly way in a fair contest!" Realizing that Ewaine was right, Gawain put up his sword.

The Black Knight did the same. "I'm glad this quarrel is over," he said, "I see, Sirs, that you're knights of great nobility and breeding. I'd rather we were friends than enemies. Please come take refreshment in my pavilion."

Ewaine said, "Thank you for your courtesy. We'll gladly go with you."

"I'm content," Gawain said, although he felt vexed and ashamed at having been thrown.

At the edge of the forest a green silk pavilion sat beneath a tree. Around the pavilion were many servants dressed in green and white. Gawain realized that the Black Knight was someone of very high estate. This thought somewhat comforted him. The knights removed their helmets. The Black Knight was very handsome, with a ruddy face and copper-colored hair. Ewaine said, "Sir, my companion is my cousin Sir Gawain, son of King Urien of Gore. I'm Ewaine, son of King Lot of Orkney. Please let us know who you are."

"I'm also of royal blood: Sir Marhaus, son of the king of Ireland."

Gawain was very glad to learn that the man who had defeated him was a prince. "Sir, you're one of the strongest knights in the world. Only one other knight has ever defeated me: my uncle King Arthur. You must come to his court. He'd be delighted to meet you. It's very possible that he'd make you a knight of the Round Table. There's no greater honor." Then Gawain remembered that he no longer was welcome at Camelot. "Oh! I can't invite you to King Arthur's court because I've been banished from there."

Marhaus asked what had happened. Ewaine told him all about the quarrel. Marhaus felt sorry for Gawain. "Sirs," he said, "I like both of you. May I become your companion in the adventures that you undertake? I don't need to stay here any longer. I was obliged to defend the ladies who defaced my shield until I had thrown seven knights in their behalf. Sir Gawain was the seventh, so I'm released from my obligation and free to go with you."

Gawain and Ewaine asked Marhaus to tell them how such a strange obligation had come about. "Some time ago I was hawking in this area," Marhaus said. "I was dressed in light outdoor attire. I had no weapons other than a small, light shield and a short sword. I came to a stone bridge that crossed a deep, rapid river. The bridge was so narrow that only one horse could cross at a time. I was partway across the bridge when I saw a knight in armor coming from the opposite direction. A proud-looking blond lady sat behind the knight. The knight yelled to me, 'Get back! Allow us to pass!' I responded, 'No, Sir Knight. Because I'm already on the bridge, I have the right of way. You'll have to wait for me to finish crossing.' The knight adopted an aggressive posture and came straight at me with the intent of either driving me back or killing me. I defended myself with my light weapons. I pushed my horse against theirs so that I drove the knight, lady, and horse off the bridge and into the water. The lady screamed. She and the knight were likely to drown because he was wearing heavy armor. At much danger to myself, I leaped off my horse and into the water to save them. I managed to bring both of them to land. Nevertheless, the lady vehemently upbraided me because her clothes were ruined. I kneeled before her and humbly asked her pardon, but she continued to upbraid me. I offered to make amends by performing some act of penance that she might request of me. My offer greatly mollified her. She said, 'Very well. Come with us.' I mounted my horse and followed her and her knight. We soon came to this place. The lady said to me, 'This castle belongs to this knight, who is my husband, and me. Hang your shield in that sycamore tree. Every day I'll send seven of my ladies out to deface your shield. In addition to suffering whatever offense they offer, you must defend them against all comers until you've thrown seven knights.'"

Gawain and Ewaine congratulated Marhaus on having done his penance. They stayed in his pavilion that night. The next morning the three knights and their squires washed themselves in a forest stream and left, traveling with no destination in mind. In the afternoon Marhaus suddenly remarked, "This is the Forest of Adventure. Whenever a knight enters it, he'll meet with some adventure."

"I'm glad we're here, then," Ewaine said.

The forest was silent and dark. No bird chirped. Hardly any light penetrated the dense foliage. Suddenly a white fawn wearing a collar of pure gold appeared in front of the knights. She stood and looked at them, but when they got closer, she turned and ran down a narrow path. Gawain said, "Let's follow the fawn and see where she goes." The three knights followed the narrow

path until they came to a small lawn bright with sunlight. In the middle of the lawn Nymue sat beside a fountain. She combed her raven-black hair with a golden comb. She was dressed in green and wore gold bracelets inset with emeralds and opals. When Nymue saw the knights, she rose, set her comb aside, and bound her hair with ribbons of scarlet silk. Then she greeted the knights.

The knights immediately dismounted. Gawain said, "Lady, I believe you're a fairy."

"Yes, Sir Gawain."

"Who are you?" he asked.

"I'm Nymue, the Lady of the Lake. I gave King Arthur his sword Excalibur. Sir Marhaus, you'll become a famous knight of the Round Table." The three knights marveled at her words. "What is it that the three of you seek in these parts?"

"We seek adventure," Gawain answered.

"I'll bring you to an adventure that Sir Gawain must undertake."

"Gladly," Gawain said.

"Take me behind you on your saddle," Nymue said, "and I'll show you the adventure." Gawain took Nymue up behind him. She brought with her a subtle fragrance that the entire forest seemed to share. Nymue directed the knights out of the forest and into open country. She brought them to a hill overlooking Ettard's castle. From a distance the travelers saw a knight in red armor battle ten knights and throw all of them but two. They didn't know that the knight was Pellias.

"That's wonderful to see," Gawain said.

Nymue smiled and said, "Wait awhile." Gawain, Ewaine, and Marhaus now were astonished to see Pellias surrender to his last two opponents. They also witnessed the scene that followed, which ended with Pellias's being tied to his horse and driven off. Nymue said to Gawain, "You'll find your adventure there, Sir Gawain."

"I'll go," Gawain said. Nymue vanished.

Chapter 21

"**I**'ve never seen anything as wondrous as Nymue," Gawain said. "Nor have I ever seen a knight surrender when he was about to win total victory over multiple opponents. I can't understand why he did that. Let's find out." The three knights and their squires rode down into the valley. As they approached the three pavilions set up in the meadow, Brandiles and Mador came toward them. There was joyful recognition on both sides. Gawain and Ewaine shook hands with Brandiles and Mador. Gawain introduced Marhaus to Brandiles and Mador, and the five knights went into Brandiles' pavilion, where they ate white bread and drank excellent wine. Gawain asked Brandiles and Mador the meaning of the strange thing that he'd witnessed. "Who is that Red Knight?"

Looking ashamed, Mador said, "Come and see."

Sensing that something disgraceful had happened, Gawain said to Ewaine and Marhaus, "Please wait here." Mador led Gawain to the white pavilion, drew aside its curtains, and said, "Go in."

Gawain saw Pellias sitting on a bed of rushes covered with sky-blue cloth. Pellias didn't look up. His head remained bowed with despair. Gawain cried out, "Is it you, Pellias? What are you doing here?" Pellias reacted with a start. He sprang to his feet and ran to the other end of the pavilion, where he turned his face to the wall. Astonished, Gawain sternly said, "I'm amazed and greatly ashamed that a knight of King Arthur's Round Table would behave as I saw you behave today. I can hardly believe that a knight of your nobility and reputation would allow himself to be taken and bound by two inferior knights. How could you submit to such indignity?" Pellias was silent. Gawain fiercely cried, "You won't answer me?" Pellias shook his head. "Either you tell me the meaning of your shameful conduct," Gawain said, "or you'll do extreme battle with me! I won't allow you to dishonor King Arthur and the Round Table. You and I have been dear friends. But unless you immediately explain yourself, I'll hold you in contempt and regard you as an enemy."

Pellias then told Gawain everything that had happened. Gawain was astounded. "I can't understand how you've become so infatuated with this lady unless she's bewitched you."

"I think I *am* bewitched," Pellias said. "I've lost all self-control. I'm entirely unable to contain my passion."

Gawain pondered the matter. After some

time he said, "I have a plan. I'll go to Lady Ettard and look into this matter. If I find that anyone has used magic against you, I'll do my best to punish them. I won't let an enchanter beguile you as one beguiled Merlin."

"How will you gain admittance to Lady Ettard?" Pellias asked.

"I'll go to the castle dressed in your armor," Gawain said. "I'll say that I defeated you in an encounter and took your armor. They'll admit me because they'll be eager to hear what happened. I'll speak to Lady Ettard."

"Very well," Pellias said.

Gawain put on Pellias's armor, mounted Pellias's horse, and rode to the castle. Ettard was walking on a balcony. She looked down and saw Gawain but thought he was Pellias. Furious, she said to those around her, "That knight vexes me so much that I fear I'll become ill if he comes here many more times. I wish I knew how to get rid of him." She beckoned to Gawain. When he had come near to the castle walls, she said, "Sir Knight, why do you keep coming here? Don't you understand that the more I see you, the more I hate you?"

Gawain opened his helmet, and Ettard saw that he wasn't Pellias. "Lady," Gawain said, "I'm wearing your enemy's armor because I've defeated him in battle. He won't bother you anymore."

Ettard was astonished that a single knight

could defeat Pellias, but she believed Gawain. She commanded servants to bring him into the castle and show him all honor because she thought he must be one of the world's greatest champions. Gawain was brought before Ettard in a large hall illuminated by seven tall windows of colored glass and decorated all around with fine tapestries. He held his helmet under his arm and against his hip. He was extraordinarily handsome. His eyes were steel blue, his nose high and curved, his hair and beard a rich dark brown. His bearing was steadfast and proud. Everyone who saw him felt awe.

Ettard gave Gawain her hand. He kneeled and put it to his lips. Ettard graciously said, "Sir Knight, please tell us your name and degree of estate."

"Lady, I can't tell you yet because I've taken a vow of secrecy. I crave your patience for a little while."

"It's a great pity that we can't know your name and degree. However, I still hope that you'll give us the pleasure of your company for a few days." Ettard was wearing the necklace that Pellias had given her. She loved it so much that she rarely took it off.

Gawain looked at the necklace, and its power took hold of him. He began to feel ardent love for Ettard, so he was very pleased to accept her invitation. Gazing at her with adoration, he said, "You're exceedingly gentle to extend such a great courtesy to me. I'll be glad beyond measure to stay with you for a while."

Ettard was very pleased. She thought, "If I can persuade this knight to remain in my court as my champion, I'll gain great credit. I'll also have someone to defend my rights." So she was gracious and charming toward Gawain.

The more favor that Ettard showed Gawain, the more distressed Engamore became. He thought, "Before these foreign knights came here, I was Lady Ettard's favorite. She was prepared to marry me. Then Sir Pellias threw me, and now this knight has thrown *him*. So I've dwindled to nothing in Lady Ettard's estimation." Engamore sorrowfully withdrew to his chamber.

Ettard and Gawain walked together in the castle's gardens. Standing some distance away, one servant commented to another, "It would be good if this knight stayed here and Lady Ettard took him as her champion."

Gawain and Ettard walked and talked cheerfully until sunset. Then they sat down to a great feast. A number of pages played the harp while various ladies sang. Gawain was delighted. "Why should I ever leave here?" he thought. "I've been banished from King Arthur's court. Why shouldn't I establish my own court here—one as glorious as his?" He found Ettard so beautiful that this thought greatly pleased him.

Meanwhile Pellias was having misgivings about Gawain's plan. He thought, "What if

Gawain forgets his duty when he meets Lady Ettard? She possesses a potent charm that might easily draw Gawain to her, especially if some magic is at work." Pellias became more and more troubled. At twilight he called a squire to him and said, "Fetch me the black hooded cloak of a Dominican friar." When it was completely dark, Pellias put on the cloak and went to the castle. Because the castle's residents believed him to be a friar, they let him in. Pellias inquired where he might find the knight who had come that afternoon.

"What do you want with him?" a servant asked.

"I have a message for him," Pellias said.

"You can't see him right now," the servant said. "He's having supper with Lady Ettard."

The thought of Gawain making merry with Ettard greatly angered Pellias. "I must speak with that knight," he said sternly. "Please bring me to him without delay."

"Wait here," the servant said. "We'll ask him if he wants to see you."

A servant went to Gawain and said, "Sir Knight, a friar wants to speak with you." Gawain wondered whether the friar was a messenger from Pellias. His conscience bothered him because he knew he wasn't behaving honorably toward his friend, so he agreed to see the friar.

Pellias was brought to a room just outside the one in which Gawain and Ettard were dining.

He peered in on Gawain and Ettard to see whether or not Gawain had betrayed him. The room in which Gawain and Ettard sat was illuminated by dozens of candles that emitted a fragrant scent. Pellias saw that Gawain and Ettard delighted in each other's company. They drank wine out of the same gold chalice. Pellias felt great anger and indignation. He entered the room and threw back his hood, showing his face. Ettard shrieked. Gawain sat silent. Pellias went up to Ettard with such a threatening expression that she froze with fear. He grabbed her necklace and yanked it with such force that the clasp broke and it came off. "This is mine!" he thundered. "You have no right to it!" He put it into his pocket. Then he turned to Gawain and said, "You've betrayed both your knighthood and our friendship." Pellias slapped Gawain so hard that red marks remained on Gawain's cheek.

Gawain cried, "Sir, I have indeed betrayed you, but you've given me such affront that our injuries now are equal."

"That isn't so," Pellias said. "I've injured only your cheek. You've injured my heart. I'll happily answer to you for the affront I've given you, but you'll also answer to *me*."

"I'm willing to answer to you in full measure," Gawain said.

"And you will," Pellias said. He turned and left without looking back.

Now that Ettard no longer wore the magic necklace, Gawain lost his attraction to her. In fact, he now strongly disliked her. "How is it possible that I betrayed my knighthood and my friend for this woman who has done him so much harm?" he thought. Gawain violently pushed back his chair and rose from the table.

Ettard angrily said, "I'm happy for you to leave. You lied to me when you said that you'd defeated Sir Pellias, who is stronger and nobler than you. He struck you as if you were his servant. Your cheek still bears the mark of his hand."

Gawain angrily replied, "I think you bewitched me. As for Sir Pellias, look down from your castle walls tomorrow and see if I don't put a deeper mark on him than he's put on me." Gawain strode to the courtyard and had servants fetch his horse. He rode out into the night, glad that he was concealed by darkness, which made his shame easier to bear. When he reached the pavilions, Ewaine and Marhaus came out and asked him to come inside. Gawain refused. He wouldn't go into the light, which would reveal the mark of Pellias's hand on his face. He told Ewaine and Marhaus to leave him alone. When they'd gone, Gawain said to his squire, "Take this armor off me, and give it to Sir Pellias." The squire removed the red armor and brought it to Pellias. Greatly troubled, Gawain stayed outside—pacing—the entire night.

Chapter 22

In the morning Gawain put on his armor and mounted his horse. The grass sparkled with dew. Birds sang joyfully. Gawain felt heartened. "Take this glove of mine to Sir Pellias," he said to his squire. "Tell him that I'm in front of the castle challenging him to combat on horse or foot—whichever way he prefers."

The squire was astonished because Gawain and Pellias had always been close friends, but he didn't comment. "Won't you eat something before you do battle?" he asked.

"No," Gawain answered.

When Pellias received the message, he said, "Tell your master that I'll come to meet him as soon as I've eaten."

Brandiles, Mador, Ewaine, and Marhaus were greatly disturbed when they learned of Gawain's challenge to Pellias. They went to see Pellias. "What's this quarrel between you and Gawain?" Ewaine asked.

"It's none of your business," Pellias replied.

"You're going to do serious battle with a friend?" Ewaine said.

"He isn't my friend anymore."

"It's a great pity that you and Gawain have quarreled," Brandiles said. "Will you let us make peace between you?"

"You can't make peace," Pellias said. The four knights left him alone.

After breakfast Pellias put on his red armor and rode to the castle. Many people had gathered on the walls. Word had spread that the knight who would fight Pellias was Sir Gawain, King Lot's son and King Arthur's nephew. Ettard stood in a tower that overlooked the field of battle. Pellias again wore the gold necklace with emeralds and opals, so when Ettard looked at him, she desired him again and hoped that he would win.

Gawain and Pellias took their places and prepared their weapons. Marhaus gave the signal, and Gawain and Pellias dashed at each other. Gawain's spear burst up to the hand guard, but Pellias's remained intact. Gawain was thrown from his saddle. He hit the ground with such force that he rolled over three times and then lay motionless. The castle spectators cheered. Brandiles, Mador, Ewaine, and Marhaus hurried to Gawain, whose squire quickly unlaced his helmet. Gawain's face was ashen. He didn't seem to be breathing. "I think you've killed him,"

Marhaus said to Pellias.

"He hasn't been punished more than he deserved," Pellias responded.

Ewaine was indignant. "You forget this knight's quality. In addition to being a fellow member of the Round Table to whom you've vowed brotherhood, he's the son of a king and the nephew of King Arthur himself."

Pellias maintained a steadfast expression. "I wouldn't regret this if he were a king himself."

Furious, Ewaine cried, "Go, or a great ill may befall you!" Pellias turned his horse and rode off into the woods. Gawain was carried to the pavilion that Pellias had occupied and placed on Pellias's couch. He remained unconscious for more than an hour, but then he revived.

Pellias had been seriously wounded. Although Gawain's spear had shattered, its head had pierced Pellias's armor and entered his side. The spear's iron tip, several inches long, had remained in Pellias's body a little above his waist. While Pellias had sat talking to the four knights, blood had been pouring into his armor. Although dizzy and in severe pain, Pellias had said nothing about his wound. However, once he was in the forest, he groaned and said out loud, "I think I've received my death wound."

That morning Parcenet had ridden out with Ettard's dwarf Gansaret to fly a young falcon. In the woods Parcenet heard Pellias's groans. She

and Gansaret followed the sound and found Pellias sitting, in his red armor, on a black horse beneath an oak tree. Pellias leaned against his spear, whose tip was lodged in the ground. Otherwise he would have fallen from his horse out of weakness. Parcenet hurried to him. "Sir Pellias, what ails you?"

Pellias saw her through a haze. "I'm badly hurt," he said weakly.

"Where?" she asked.

"In my side. There's a spear point inside me. I think I'm dying."

Parcenet cried out in sorrow. Gansaret said, "Damsel, a holy hermit lives in this forest. He's a skillful doctor. If we can get Sir Pellias to the hermit, he might be saved." The hermit to which Gansaret referred was the same hermit who had cared for King Arthur after he had been badly wounded by Pellinore.

Parcenet said to Gansaret, "Let's take him right away."

Gansaret took Pellias's horse by the bridle and led him through the forest. Parcenet rode beside Pellias, holding him up in his saddle. Pellias fainted from sickness and pain. Because they had to travel slowly, the group didn't reach the hermit's dwelling until noon. Parcenet looked at the small chapel among the trees. Around it was a small flowery lawn. A clear fountain was near the door. In front of the chapel a wild doe and her fawn browsed on the tender grass and foliage without any fear of harm. When Parcenet, Gansaret, and Pellias approached, the doe and fawn looked up with widened eyes and spread their ears, but they didn't flee. They soon returned to browsing. Around the chapel many birds chirped in the trees. They were waiting for the midday meal that the hermit always gave them. At noon a bell in the chapel sounded sweetly. Parcenet and Gansaret crossed themselves. When the bell stopped ringing, Gansaret called, "Hello! Someone here needs help!"

The hermit opened his door and came out. Many birds flew around him, expecting to be fed.

The hermit gently waved them away and went up to the travelers. "Who are you?" he asked. "Why have you come here with this wounded knight?"

Parcenet explained, and the hermit agreed to take Pellias in. After helping to lay Pellias on the hermit's couch, Parcenet and Gansaret headed home.

The hermit examined Pellias's wound. Pellias lay unconscious and near death. "I can't save him," the hermit thought. He prepared the last sacrament.

The door opened, and Nymue entered. She went to Pellias and leaned over him so that her breath touched his forehead. "Oh!" she exclaimed.

"Yes, Lady," the hermit said. "This knight with live only a few minutes more."

"That isn't so, holy man. He's going to live a long time yet." Nymue removed the necklace that she had given to Pellias and put it around her own neck.

"Why do you take that from a dying man?" the hermit asked.

"I gave it to him," Nymue said calmly, "so I'm only taking back what's mine. Please leave me alone with this knight for a little while. I think I can save him."

"Are you going to use magic?" the hermit asked.

"Yes, but it won't be black magic," Nymue said.

Reassured, the hermit left Nymue alone with Pellias. Nymue took out a magic loadstone and placed it against Pellias's wound. The spearhead came out. Pellias groaned, and much blood spurted out. Nymue held a fine linen cloth against the wound, and the bleeding stopped. Next she took from her bosom a small crystal vial filled with a fragrant blue potion. She poured some of the potion between Pellias's cold lips. Life reentered his body. He opened his eyes and gazed around. Upon seeing Nymue, he thought that he had died and gone to heaven. "Am I dead?" he asked.

"No," Nymue said, "but you've come perilously close."

"Where am I?"

"In the hut of a saintly hermit."

"Who brought me back to life?" Pellias asked.

"I did."

Pellias lay silent for a time. Then he said, "I feel strange."

"That's because you're different now. To save your life I gave you a potion that made you half mortal and half fairy."

Pellias saw that Nymue was wearing the necklace she had given to him. He felt strong love for her. "Please let me always be near you."

"It was for that purpose that I let you nearly die and then made you half fairy," Nymue said.

She went out and soon returned with an earthen crock filled with water from the fountain. "Drink some water now."

When Pellias drank, he felt his strength returning. But he was physically very different from before. His body felt as light as air. He felt more joy than ever before. Rising, he said, "You've given me new life. I pledge my life to you forever."

Nymue smiled at Pellias with much love. "Sir Pellias, I've held you in tender regard ever since I first saw you when you were young. You were in this forest. The day was hot. You set aside your helmet, and a young milkmaid, brown-faced and barefoot, gave you a bowl of milk, which you drank with relish. Ever since, I've felt great friendship for King Arthur and his court, for your sake."

"Lady, will you accept me as your knight?"

"Yes."

"May I kiss you?"

"Yes," Nymue said.

Pellias kissed her on the lips, and their betrothal was pledged.

Before reaching the castle, Parcenet and Gansaret came upon Mador in half armor. "Sir Mador!" Parcenet called out. "I've just come from a hermit's hut where I left Sir Pellias so badly wounded that he's almost sure to die."

"What!" Mador cried. "When Sir Pellias left

us this morning, he gave no sign of being wounded."

"He has a spearhead in his side," Parcenet said.

"This is sad news," Mador said. "Please excuse me." He hurried to the pavilions and told his companions the news.

Gawain had completely recovered from his fall. When he heard the news, he lamented, "Oh! What have I done? First I betrayed my friend, and now I've slain him. I must beg his forgiveness before he dies."

Ewaine protested, "You aren't well enough to travel yet."

"I don't care," Gawain said. "I must go to my friend." He insisted on going alone.

Shortly before sunset, when the light fell as red as fire through the forest leaves, Gawain came to the hermit's hut. The hermit was outside digging in a small lentil garden. At Gawain's approach he stopped and leaned on his trowel. Gawain told the hermit why he had come. "A fairy came several hours ago," the hermit said. "She cured your friend through magic. The two rode away into the forest."

Gawain was greatly surprised and relieved. "Please tell me which way they went."

"Westward," the hermit answered.

Gawain rode off in pursuit. As twilight fell, a pale-blue knight miraculously appeared before

Gawain and showed him the way. After following the knight for a long time, Gawain emerged from the forest onto a vast plain. The plain was illuminated by a pale silver light like that of a full moon, but there was no moon shining that night. Gawain could see everything with wonderful distinctness. The plain was covered with flowers whose scents filled the night. In front of him was a wide, still lake. Gawain rode through the tall flowers toward the lake. He felt somewhat afraid because he knew he'd entered a magical place.

As Gawain neared the lake, Pellias and Nymue approached him. Gawain was overjoyed to see Pellias alive. He galloped up to Pellias, jumped off his horse, and cried, "Forgive me!" He would have embraced Pellias, but Pellias withdrew from contact, although not angrily.

Pellias spoke in a clear, thin voice that sounded as if it came from a distance. "Don't touch me. I'm part fairy now. I forgive you for any injury I suffered at your hands. I also give you my love. I greatly hope for your happiness. But now I must leave you, dear friend. I probably won't see you again. Please return to King Arthur's court, make peace with Queen Guinevere, and tell them everything that has happened to me."

"I will," Gawain promised. He sorrowfully asked, "Where are you going?"

"To the wonderful city of gold and sky blue that lies in that valley of flowers."

"I don't see any city," Gawain said. "I see only a lake."

"Nevertheless, there's a city there," Pellias said. "Farewell."

Gawain looked into Pellias's face, which shone with a strange light. Pellias's skin was like ivory and his eyes like bright jewels. His smile never changed, as is true of fairies. Pellias and Nymue turned and rode toward the lake. When their horses stepped into the water, Pellias and Nymue vanished. Gawain stood where he was a long time, weeping.

Gawain kept his promise to Pellias. He returned to Arthur's court, made peace with Guinevere, and told Pellias's story. Everyone marveled at the tale.

Marhaus became a knight of the Round Table. Ettard took Engamore back into her favor; they married, and Engamore became lord of Grantmesnle.

Chapter 23

In the summer, King Arthur, Queen Guinevere, and a court of more than 120 people traveled in great state through a part of Arthur's kingdom far from Camelot. At midday Arthur commanded that pavilions be set up in a pleasant glade so that everyone could rest during the hottest part of the day. Tables were set out in the shade of trees. A gentle breeze blew. Many birds sang. Everyone sat down to feast.

A white buck and white hound, each wearing a collar of gold, burst from the forest cover. The hound pursued the buck with much baying. The buck fled in terror. The two ran three times around the table at which Arthur sat eating. Twice the hound nipped the buck in his haunch, drawing blood. But each time the buck escaped. He fled into the forest, still pursued by the hound, whose baying became more and more faint.

A knight and lady appeared where the buck and hound had appeared. The knight was in half armor and rode a dappled gray horse. The lady wore green hunting attire and rode a spotted horse. With them were two squires, also dressed for the chase. Seeing the great gathering, the hunters paused in surprised.

An angry-looking armored knight on a black horse now appeared. He rode up to the half-armed knight and struck him with his sword, knocking him from his horse. The lady screamed. The fully armed knight rode up to the lady, lifted her from her horse, laid her across the horn of his saddle, and rode back into the forest while the lady screamed. The two squires lifted the wounded knight onto his horse, and the three went back into the forest.

Arthur and his court watched all of this from too great a distance to intervene. The incident puzzled and disturbed them. Arthur said to his knights, "Sirs, will one of you pursue the knight on the black horse and compel him to defend his behavior?"

Gawain said, "Lord, I'll gladly do that. May I take Gaheris along as my squire? He's growing into manhood, yet he's never seen a considerable adventure at arms."

"You may take him with you," Arthur said.

Gawain and his younger brother Gaheris eagerly rode off in the direction in which the buck had fled. Every so often they encountered forest folk and asked them if they'd seen a white hound, white buck, or knight with a captive lady.

Late in the afternoon, Gawain and Gaheris heard an uproar. They followed the noise, which brought them to a meadow in which two knights were fighting fiercely. As Gawain and Gaheris approached, the two knights paused in their encounter. "Sirs, why are you fighting so fiercely?" Gawain asked.

"Sir, this matter doesn't concern you," one knight answered.

"Don't meddle with us," the other said.

"I won't interfere in your quarrel," Gawain said. "I'm in pursuit of a white buck and white hound who came this way, and of a knight who has carried off a lady. Have you seen any of them?"

One knight answered, "We're fighting over that very matter. I'm Sir Sorloise, and this is my brother Sir Brian. We were riding in good fellowship when the buck and hound crossed our path. My brother said he greatly hoped that the white buck would escape. I said I hoped that the hound would bring the buck down. Then the knight with the captive lady passed by. I said that I'd follow him and rescue the lady. My brother said that *he'd* do that. We ended up fighting as you see."

"I can't understand how such a serious fight arose from such a small dispute," Gawain said. "It's a pity for brothers to quarrel and give each other wounds, which I see you've both received."

"You're right," Brian said. "I feel ashamed."

Sorloise said, "I'm also sorry for what I've

done. Please do us the honor of telling us who you are."

When Gawain told them his name and position, Brian and Sorloise were astonished and excited. "It's a joy to meet a knight as famous as you, Sir Gawain," Brian said.

"Sir Knights, a short time ago the buck and hound appeared where King Arthur, Queen Guinevere, and their court were picnicking. We also saw the knight capture the lady. At King Arthur's command my brother Gaheris and I set out to discover the incident's meaning. I'd consider it a great courtesy if you'd stop fighting, go to King Arthur, and tell him what has happened. Otherwise I'll have to fight you both—at considerable disadvantage to you because you're weary from battle whereas I'm fresh."

Sorloise said, "We'll do as you wish. We have no desire to fight as powerful a knight as you." They set off to report to King Arthur.

Gawain and Gaheris rode on. Upon reaching a large river they saw a knight riding in full armor. He carried a spear; a shield hung from his saddle bow. Gawain hurried forward, calling out. The knight stopped and waited for Gawain to reach him. "Sir Knight," Gawain asked, "have you seen a white buck and white hound pass by, or a knight carrying a captive lady?"

"Yes, I saw all of them," the knight said. "In fact, I'm following them now."

"Please let me be the one to pursue this," Gawain said.

"Sir," the other knight said angrily, "I don't know who you are, and I don't much care. I intend to see this through and won't permit anyone to stop me."

"Sir," Gawain said, "you won't proceed unless you deal with me first."

"Very well," the knight said.

Each knight prepared for combat. Then they rushed at each other. The spear of the strange knight shattered, but Gawain's remained intact. The strange knight was hurled to the ground. He lay unconscious. Gawain rode up to him and removed his helmet. The knight was young and handsome. He regained consciousness, and Gawain asked, "Do you yield to me?"

"Yes," the knight said.

"Who are you?"

"Sir Alardin of the Isles."

"Sir Alardin, I command you to go to King Arthur's court and deliver yourself to him as a captive of my prowess. Tell him everything that has happened." Alardin agreed, and they parted.

Gawain and Gaheris rode on. Toward sunset they came upon the body of the white hound. It was lying beside the road, pierced by three arrows. "What a pity that this beautiful and noble hound was slain this way!" Gawain exclaimed. "Whoever killed him must have been protecting

the white buck. If I find the buck, I'll slay him."
Gawain and Gaheris soon saw the buck browsing
on the green in front of a castle. As soon as the
buck saw them, he fled into the courtyard. Gawain
and Gaheris raced in pursuit. They cornered the
buck. Gawain leaped from his horse, drew his
sword, and slew the buck with a single blow.

Having heard the commotion, the castle's lord
and lady—Sir Ablamor and Lady Constance—
came out. Ablamor looked noble and proud.
Constance was graceful and beautiful. When she
saw that the buck lay dead on the courtyard's
pavement, she screamed. "Oh! My beloved deer,
are you dead?" she cried. Then she sobbed.

"Lady, I'm very sorry for what I've done. I
wish I could undo it," Gawain said.

"Are you the one who killed the buck?"
Ablamor asked Gawain.

"Yes."

"Sir, you've done very ill. If you'll wait a little, I'll take revenge on you."

"I'll wait as long as you wish," Gawain
responded.

Ablamor went to his chamber, put on armor,
and returned to the courtyard. Without any
warning he struck Gawain with his sword. It cut
through Gawain's shoulder armor and went
through his flesh and into his bone. Gawain was
in agony. Enraged, he cut through Ablamor's
helmet and into his skull. Ablamor collapsed to

his knees. Gawain snatched off his helmet. "Sir Knight," Ablamor said weakly, "I beg for mercy and yield to you." Still furious, Gawain lifted his sword to slay Ablamor.

Constance ran forward and flung herself on Ablamor, shielding him with her body. Gawain turned his sword to avoid hitting Constance but still struck her neck with the flat of his sword. The blade cut her a little. Blood ran down her smooth, white neck. She fell unconscious. Fearing that he had killed her, Gawain lamented, "Oh! What have I done?"

"You've struck a shameful blow," Gaheris said. "As your brother, I share your shame. I wish I'd never come with you."

Believing that his wife was dead, Ablamor cried, "I no longer want your mercy! Since you've slain my lady, who was dearer to me than my own life, you might as well slay me too. I'd consider it a favor."

Ladies ran to Constance. One of them said to Ablamor, "She isn't dead! She only has fainted." Ablamor wept with joy. Gawain came to him, lifted him up from the ground, and kissed him on the cheek. Others carried Constance to her chamber, where she soon recovered.

That night Gawain and Gaheris stayed at the castle. When Ablamor learned who Gawain was, he felt honored to host such a famous knight. So they feasted together in friendship. Afterwards

Gawain said, "Sir Ablamor, please tell me how the white hound came to pursue the white deer."

"I have a brother whom I've always loved," Ablamor began. "When I married Lady Constance, he married her sister. My brother lives in a nearby castle, and we often spent time together. One day my wife and her sister were riding and talking when a strange but beautiful lady appeared before them. She had a white buck and a white hound, each on a silver leash attached to a gold collar. She gave the white buck to my wife and the white hound to my sister-in-law. My wife and sister-in-law were delighted. Ever since, however, there's been nothing but discord between my brother and me, and between my wife and sister-in-law. The hound has continually tried to kill the deer, so my wife and I have been very offended that my brother and sister-in-law have failed to keep the hound at home. A number of times we've tried to kill the hound, so that my brother and sister-in-law have taken equal offense against *us*. Today when I was in the forest, I heard a great cry. The white buck came fleeing through the woods, with the white hound in pursuit. My brother and sister-in-law rapidly followed. I was greatly angered because I thought they were hunting the buck, so I followed them with all speed. I caught up with my brother at the forest's outskirts, near some pavilions, and struck him such a blow that he fell from his horse. I then grabbed my sister-in-law, threw her across the horn of my saddle, and brought her here as a captive. My lady loved that buck more than anything else in the world except me."

"What did the lady who gave your wife the buck look like?"

"She was dressed all in crimson and wore gold necklaces and bracelets set with various gems. Her hair was reddish gold and in a gold net. Her eyes were black and shining. Her lips were like coral."

"Ha!" Gawain said. "I think she was the sorceress Vivien, who spends all of her time doing harm out of pure spite. It would be good if someone killed her. But tell me: where is your sister-in-law now?"

"She's a prisoner in the castle."

"Well, now that both the buck and the hound are dead, you shouldn't bear your brother and sister-in-law any ill will. I beseech you to free your sister-in-law and restore peace in your family."

Ablamor said, "I'll do as you advise." And he did.

The next day Gawain and Gaheris returned to Arthur's court and related everything that had happened. Guinevere was very displeased when she heard that Gawain had refused to show Ablamor mercy and had struck Constance. "Any sword that strikes a woman is dishonored, and any knight who strikes a woman breaks his vow of knighthood," Guinevere said to the person standing next to her. Gawain overheard.

When Gawain was alone with Gaheris, he said, "The queen hates me. She considers me discourteous and ungentle. Since she considers my sword dishonored, I won't use it anymore." He took the sword from its sheath, broke it across his knee, and threw away the pieces.

Chapter 24

In the spring, King Arthur went to Tintagel on state business. Queen Guinevere and the court went to Carleon, where they waited for Arthur to join them.

One especially pleasant day Arthur summoned his favorite squire and said, "Boisenard, let's go to Carleon without telling anyone. My arrival will be a surprise for the queen." Arthur put on armor with no coat of arms, and he and Boisenard rode off without telling anyone where they were going. Arthur whistled, sang, and joked. He was as merry as a colt let loose in a pasture on a glorious spring day. Because they wandered around taking pleasure in the countryside, Arthur and Boisenard became lost in the woods. When night fell, Arthur said, "Boisenard, I don't know where we'll find lodging."

"Lord, with your permission I'll climb a tree and see if I can detect any habitation."

"Do that," Arthur said.

Boisenard climbed a very tall tree. From the

top he saw a faraway light. He came down, and he and Arthur rode toward the light. Eventually they reached a grim-looking castle. They rode up, and Boisenard called out and knocked at the gate. A porter came and asked what they wanted. "We're weary and seek lodging for the night," Boisenard said.

"Who are you?" the porter said roughly.

"This is a knight of good quality, and I'm his squire. We've lost our way and need shelter."

"If you're wise, you'll sleep in the forest sooner than come here. This isn't a good place for traveling knights to seek shelter."

"We demand to lodge here," Arthur said.

"Very well. Come in." The porter opened the gate, and Arthur and Boisenard rode into the courtyard. Many lights came on within the castle. Servants came running. They helped Arthur and Boisenard dismount, took their horses, and brought basins of water so that Arthur and Boisenard could wash their face and hands. Then Arthur and Boisenard were led into the castle. They heard talking, laughter, singing, and harp music. Many people were feasting in the castle's hall, which was lit by candles and torches. At the head of the table sat a bearded knight with white hair. Although elderly, he looked very strong, with a broad chest and shoulders. He also looked stern and forbidding. He was dressed all in black, and he wore a gold chain necklace with a gold locket. He called to Arthur and Boisenard that they should come and sit with him at the head of the table. Others moved aside, and Arthur and Boisenard sat beside the host, who spoke to them pleasantly while they ate with relish.

After the feasting the host said to Arthur, "Sir, you're young, strong, and apparently brave. What do you say to a little sport between us?" His eyes sparkled.

"Sir, what sport do you have in mind?"

The host laughed. "Each of us will prove his courage."

"How so?" Arthur asked.

"You and I will stand in the middle of this hall, and you'll try to strike my head off. If I can receive your blow without dying, I'll try to strike *your* head off."

Arthur felt dread. "That's a very strange kind of sport."

Some people burst out laughing. "Are you afraid?" the host asked.

"No," Arthur said angrily. "No one has ever had reason to say that I feared anyone."

"Let's begin, then," the host said.

Boisenard whispered to Arthur, "Lord, let me undertake this in your place. I fear that some great treachery is planned."

"No, Boisenard," Arthur said. "No man will take my danger upon himself." Then Arthur said to the host, "I'm ready."

The host rose and laid aside his black robe. He wore a fine linen shirt and crimson stockings. He opened his shirt at the throat and turned down his collar, baring his neck. "Sir Knight, you'll have to strike well to win at this sport."

Arthur drew Excalibur. He measured his distance, lifted the sword, and smote the host on the neck with all his might. The host's head flew from his body and fell a considerable distance away. But the host's body remained standing. It walked over to the head, picked it up, and set it back on the body. The host was as whole and sound as before! Clearly he was a wizard. The gathering cheered, laughed, and shouted to Arthur, "Your turn!"

Arthur laid aside his outer tunic and opened his shirt at the throat. Boisenard grieved. "Are you afraid?" the wizard asked.

"No," Arthur said. "Every man dies. It appears that my time has come and that I'm going to lose my life in this foolish way."

"Stand back a little," the wizard said, "so that I can strike you from the right distance." Arthur stood back. The wizard swung his sword several times but didn't strike. Several times he laid the cold blade on Arthur's neck.

Arthur angrily said, "It's your right to strike but not to torment me."

"No," the wizard responded, "it's my right to strike when it pleases me to do so. If it pleases

me, I'll torment you a long time before I slay you." He laid his sword on Arthur's neck several more times. Arthur remained silent, with a steadfast expression. "You appear to be very brave and honorable," the wizard said. "I think I'll make a covenant with you."

"What covenant?" Arthur asked.

"I'll spare your life for a year if you'll give me your word of honor to return here a year from now." Arthur swore on the cross of Excalibur's hilt. "I'll make another covenant with you," the wizard said.

"What is it?"

"I'll give you a riddle. If you answer it correctly when you return here, I'll spare your life and set you free."

"What's the riddle?" Arthur asked.

"The riddle is this: What do women most desire?"

"I'll try to find the answer. Thank you for giving me the chance to escape death," Arthur said.

The wizard smiled sourly. "I'm not offering this out of mercy but because I enjoy tormenting you. What happiness can you have living your life in the knowledge that you'll soon die?"

"You're very cruel," Arthur said.

"I don't deny that."

Arthur and Boisenard stayed in the castle that night and left the next day. Arthur was very troubled. He told Boisenard not to tell anyone what had happened.

During the next year Arthur settled his affairs. He also looked everywhere for an answer to the riddle. People gave him many answers. Some said that women chiefly desire wealth.

Some said beauty. Some said the power to please others. No answer seemed right to Arthur. When only two weeks remained until he must return to the wizard's castle, Arthur said, "Boisenard, help me to arm. I'm going away."

"Lord, don't go," Boisenard pleaded.

Arthur looked sternly at Boisenard and said, "Would you tempt me to break my word? It isn't hard to die, but it would be very hard to live without honor. If I don't return within a month, tell everyone what has happened, and tell Sir Constantine to look through the papers in my cabinet. They lay out everything that should be done upon my death."

Weeping, Boisenard put a plain suit of armor on Arthur. The king's outer tunic and shield also had no coat of arms. Arthur rode off.

Along the way Arthur asked everyone he met what women most desire. No answer seemed right. The day before his promised return to the wizard's castle, Arthur wandered through the adjacent forest in despair. He came across a small hut under an oak tree. Smoke rose from the hut. Arthur opened the door and entered. He saw an old woman sitting bent over a small fire that burned on the hearth. Arthur never had seen such an ugly woman. Her ears were huge. Her hair hung like snakes. Her face was covered with wrinkles. Her eyes were coated with a film. Her eyelids were red as if from continual weeping.

She had only one tooth in her mouth. Her hands, which she spread out to the fire, were like claws.

Arthur greeted her, and she returned the greeting. "My lord king, why have you come here?"

Arthur was astonished that the old woman knew who he was. "Who are you?" he asked. "How do you know me?"

"I'm someone who means you well," she answered. "Tell me what brings you here."

Arthur told her everything and asked, "Do you know the answer to the riddle?"

"Yes," she said, "but I won't tell you unless you promise me something."

"What is it?" he asked.

"When you return home, you must let me choose any knight of your court to be my husband."

"How can I promise such a thing without the other person's consent?"

"Aren't your knights noble enough to marry me in order to honor a promise that saved your life?"

"I believe that they are," Arthur said. He thought, "What will become of my kingdom if I die now? I have no right to sacrifice my life." So he said, "Very well. I'll make that promise."

"This is the answer to the riddle," the old woman said. "What women most desire is to have their way." The answer seemed entirely right to Arthur. "The knight who has placed you in this situation is an evil magician," the woman said. "His life doesn't reside within his body but within a crystal globe that he wears in a locket on his necklace. If you destroy that locket—and only if you do that—he'll die."

"I'll remember that," Arthur said.

The woman gave Arthur good food and drink, and he stayed in her hut that night. The next morning he set out for the wizard's castle. He was more cheerful than he'd been in a year.

Chapter 25

When Arthur arrived at the castle, the gate was immediately opened. Servants led him into the main hall. Arthur saw the wizard and many people who had come to witness the end of the adventure. "Sir, have you come to fulfill your promise?" the wizard asked Arthur.

"Yes."

"Have you guessed the riddle?"

"I think so," Arthur answered.

"Let me hear your answer. If you're wrong, you'll die."

"What women most desire is to have their way."

Everyone was silent, knowing that Arthur had given the correct answer. Arthur went up to the wizard and sternly said, "Now it's my turn to propose a game. Give me your necklace, and I'll give you mine." The wizard paled. Arthur grabbed him by the arm and tore his necklace off. The wizard shrieked, fell to his knees, and pleaded for mercy. The gathering broke into an uproar. Arthur opened the locket. There was the crystal ball. "I'll have no mercy," Arthur said. He flung the ball down onto the stone floor. It smashed. The wizard gave a piercing cry and fell to the floor, dead.

The people of the castle feared Arthur, who stood in kingly majesty. He turned and left. No one hindered his departure.

Arthur went straight to the hut of the old woman. "You've helped me in my hour of need," he said. "Now I'll fulfill my promise to you. I'll take you to my court, where you'll choose one of my knights to be your husband. I think that every knight in my court will be glad to reward the person who has saved my life."

Arthur lifted the woman onto his horse, mounted, and rode off. He treated her with as much consideration and respect as he would show to the most beautiful queen. They reached the court, at Carleon, about midday. Guinevere was outside, with ladies and lords, enjoying the pleasant May weather. When Arthur approached, everyone was astonished to see an old, hideous woman riding with him. "Why is that woman with you?" Guinevere asked as he rode up. "Is this a jest?"

"This woman saved my life," Arthur said.

Everyone marveled at the king's words. "What has happened?" Guinevere asked.

Arthur told the amazing story. Then he said to the seventeen knights who were present, "I promised this aged woman that whichever one of you she chooses will marry her. Was I right to make that promise?"

All of the knights answered, "Yes, lord."

Then Arthur said to the old woman, "Lady, which knight do you choose for your husband?"

With her long, bony finger the old woman pointed to Gawain. "I choose that knight. His gold necklace, the gold circlet on his head, and his noble, proud demeanor tell me that he's the son of a king."

"Sir Gawain, are you willing to fulfill my promise to this woman?" Arthur asked.

"Yes, lord," Gawain answered. He went to the old woman, took her hand, and kissed it. Everyone went into the castle. Except for the old woman, all were silent and downcast. The old woman was given rooms in the castle, a court fit for a queen, and queenly clothes. In her magnificent robes she looked ten times uglier than before.

After eleven days Gawain married the old woman, with great pomp and ceremony, in the king's chapel. All of the guests were sorrowful. After the ceremony Gawain and his wife went to his house. Because he was greatly humiliated, Gawain shut himself in and wouldn't accept any visitors. The rest of the day he paced in his chamber. He felt such shame and despair that he considered suicide. When night came, he thought, "It's a disgrace for me to behave this way. I've married this lady. She's my wife. I'm not treating her with the regard to which she's entitled." Gawain went to his wife's rooms. She upbraided him, "You've treated me badly on our wedding day. You've stayed away from me all afternoon."

"I was troubled with many cares, but I beg your forgiveness for having neglected you," Gawain said.

"It's very dark here," his wife said.

"I'll fetch lights for you." Gawain soon returned with two tapers in gold candlesticks. His wife was sitting at the room's far end. Gawain went toward her. She rose. When the light fell on her, Gawain cried out in amazement. Instead of an old, ugly woman he saw a young woman of extraordinary beauty. Her hair was long, black, and glossy. Her eyes were black. Her lips were like coral, her teeth like pearls. Gawain was speechless. Then he said, "Who are you?" The lady didn't answer but smiled with such love that Gawain thought she might be an angel. "Where's my wife?"

"I'm your wife," the lady said.

"That's impossible! She's extremely ugly whereas you're the most beautiful woman I've ever seen."

"This is my true appearance. I've been under an evil spell. Because you married me of your own free will and with great courtesy, that spell has been weakened. For half of each day I'll appear as you see me now. For the other half I'll look like an ugly old woman."

Gawain was overjoyed. He felt passionate love for the lady. He fell to his knees, took her hands, and fervidly kissed them.

"Come sit beside me," the lady said. "Let's decide which part of the day I'll be beautiful."

"I'd like you to have this appearance at night," Gawain said, "because then we're alone together and can love each other as husband and wife."

The lady emphatically said, "I wish otherwise. Every woman cares how the world regards her. I want to appear beautiful to the world instead of enduring scorn and contempt."

"Lady, I would have it the other way," Gawain said.

"Well, I would have it *my* way," his wife said.

"So be it, then. Because you're my wife, I'll respect your wishes in all things. You'll have your way in this and all other things."

Gawain's wife laughed joyfully. "This was a last test. I'll always appear as I do now."

Gawain was overjoyed. He and his wife sat together, hand in hand. "Who are you?" Gawain asked again.

"I'm Nyneve, one of Nymue's sisters. I became mortal and left my beautiful home for your sake. You've been in my heart for a long time. I was nearby when you said farewell to Sir

Pellias beside the lake. I saw you weep when he left you. My heart went out to you with pity. When I learned of King Arthur's trouble, I had him bring me to you so that I could test your nobility. I've found you to be truly noble. Although I appeared aged, ugly, and foul, you treated me with courtesy and kindness. So it gives me great joy to have you as my husband."

"I also feel joy." Gawain put his hand on Nyneve's shoulder. They kissed.

Gawain summoned everyone in the house. They all came running. Gawain commanded his servants to bring lights and refreshments. In the light everyone saw Nyneve's beauty and felt wonder and joy. A great feast was prepared, and music was played. Hearing the festivities from a distance, members of Arthur's court said, "It's very strange that Sir Gawain should celebrate his marriage to the old woman."

The next morning Nyneve wore a dress of yellow silk, many strands of precious stones, and a gold crown. She and Gawain rode to Arthur's court. When the king, queen, and court saw Nyneve and heard everything that had happened, they rejoiced.

Afterword

About the Author

Like his character King Arthur, Howard Pyle was exceptionally fortunate: popular, loved, wealthy, successful, famous, and influential.

Born in Wilmington, Delaware in 1853, Howard was the first child of William and Margaret Pyle. William owned a leather business. Margaret had considered a career in literature or art. She loved books and illustrations, and Howard would too.

As a teenager, the fictional Arthur trains for knighthood, serving as his older brother's squire. Howard underwent his own apprenticeship. Starting at age sixteen, he attended a small, private art school in Philadelphia for three years; he studied under artist Van der Weilen. Just as Arthur quickly surpasses his brother in ability and reputation, Howard soon outshone his teacher.

Arthur easily pulls a sword from an anvil the first time he tries. A mere eighteen, he becomes king of Britain. Howard, too, had immediate success. In 1876, *Scribner's Monthly* published the first work he ever submitted for publication: an illustrated group of verses. Howard became a regular contributor of stories and drawings to a number of major New York magazines.

The imaginary Arthur is tall, handsome, and of strong build. So was Howard. Arthur falls in love with Guinevere at first sight. Howard was smitten with Anne Poole as soon as they met. Only a few weeks later, they became engaged. Like Guinevere, Anne was tall, slender, and beautiful. Arthur and Guinevere joyously marry, with everyone's hearty approval. In 1881, Howard and Anne did the same. They would have seven children.

Howard's first book, *The Merry Adventures of Robin Hood* (1883), quickly became a children's classic. Howard was the illustrator as well as author. He wrote and illustrated other popular books in rapid succession.

King Arthur and Queen Guinevere live in great comfort and splendor, often give feasts, and have many servants. Howard "lived like a king." He ate gourmet food and wore fine clothes. He and Anne gave frequent dinner parties in their large Wilmington home. Their servants and assistants included, among others, a nanny, a cook, a butler, a gardener, and three maids.

In 1894, Howard began teaching illustration at the Drexel Institute of Arts and Sciences in Philadelphia. His illustration classes soon gained a reputation as the best in the country. In 1900,

Howard resigned from Drexel to start his own art school in Wilmington, with summer classes in nearby Chadds Ford, Pennsylvania. Located in the scenic Brandywine river valley, the school was a small artists' colony rather than a conventional school. In Wilmington the students lived and worked in a building next to Howard's studio and only a brief walk from his home. In Chadds Ford they occupied buildings near the Pyle family's summer residence, a rented mansion. The school became a Camelot of training in illustration. Just as the best knights join King Arthur's court, especially talented artists attended Howard's school. Like a seat at Arthur's Round Table, a place in the school was highly competitive and highly prized.

Published in 1903, *The Story of King Arthur and His Knights* was yet another Pyle success. Two other books based on the Arthur legends soon followed: *The Story of the Champions of the Round Table* (1905) and *The Story of Sir Launcelot and His Companions* (1907). Appropriately, Howard's last book was *The Story of the Grail and the Passing of Arthur* (1910). Howard himself died a year later. Shortly after moving to Florence, Italy with his family, he succumbed to a kidney infection. He was fifty-eight.

Howard's published work was voluminous: nineteen books, thirteen of them for children; nearly two hundred magazine pieces, including many history articles; and more than three thousand illustrations. He also painted a number of murals, such as a Civil War battle scene for Minnesota's capitol. Reflecting the breadth of his talents and interests, Howard's wide circle of friends included artists, writers, and political leaders—among them, Frederic Remington, Mark Twain, Theodore Roosevelt, and Woodrow Wilson.

Howard's work was central to America's golden age of illustration. Like the legend of King Arthur, it continues to excite the imagination and influence the arts.

About the Book

The title of *King Arthur and His Knights* suggests a male-dominated world. However, the book's main female characters exert considerable power. Whereas the book's primary male characters continually fight other men to maintain their self-esteem, reputation, position, and wealth, the female characters influence events with relative ease.

Arthur's battle prowess depends partly on female assistance. Merlin tells Arthur about Excalibur, but it's the fairy Nymue, the Lady of the Lake, who enables Arthur to obtain that magical sword. Thanks to Excalibur, Arthur defeats Sir Pellinore, who becomes his ally and subordinate.

Nor are men the only ones with physical courage. When Sir Gawain is about to deal her husband a death blow, Lady Constance rushes forward to shield her husband with her own body. Unlike the belligerent courage often displayed by the book's men, her courage arises from a desire to save a life, not take one.

Female characters repeatedly save men's lives. Pellinore badly wounds Arthur, who lies near death even after the saintly hermit has treated his wounds. Arthur begins to recover only when Lady Guinevere has her personal physician apply balsam to his wounds. Similarly, the hermit can't save Sir Pellias after Pellias fights Gawain. Nymue saves Pellias. Unless Arthur correctly answers a riddle posed by an evil wizard, the wizard will kill him. Nymue's sister Nyneve gives Arthur the answer and tells him how to kill the wizard. When Sir Accolon is about to kill Arthur, the sorceress Vivien intervenes, casting a spell that makes Accolon drop Excalibur. She heals Arthur's wounds by applying an ointment that she denies to Accolon, who dies.

Female magic is powerful. Sorceress Morgan le Fay can "work her will on all things alive or inanimate." Through cunning and magic, Vivien kills Merlin, reputed to be the world's wisest man and most powerful wizard.

Some women are rulers with extensive property. Lady Ettard rules Grantmesnle and owns all of its land. Morgan rules the island of Avalon, which no one can near without her permission. Queens exercise considerable authority even when their husband is the one who rules. When Guinevere and Gawain exchange heated words, Guinevere prevails. "I've never heard anyone else reply to their queen as you've replied to me," she says. "This is my court. In it I command." She banishes Gawain.

Men continually seek women's favor. Again and again, knights engage in potentially deadly combat to defend, honor, or impress women. Arthur fights Duke Mordaunt partly to protect Guinevere. He tells her, "Your favor means more to me than anything else in the world." Arthur defeats

Geraint, then Gawain, then Ewaine, then Pellias in single combat and orders each of them to serve Guinevere for seven days. Who is more beautiful: Guinevere or Ettard? Guinevere, Pellias asserts. Ettard, Sir Engamore maintains. Guinevere herself considers the issue trivial, yet Pellias goes off to fight Engamore over the matter. Pellias, Engamore, and Gawain then contend for Ettard's favor.

Men, but not women, make fools of themselves due to sexual desire. The elderly Merlin is so strongly attracted to the teenage Vivien (who loathes him) that he follows her wherever she goes. His infatuation makes him the butt of jokes. Pellias intensely desires Ettard. At her orders he's brought outside, asleep and wearing only his undergarments, and left in front of her castle for everyone to see. Pellias's humiliation doesn't cool his ardor. "I've lost all self-control," he says. "I'm entirely unable to contain my passion." Ettard further shames Pellias by having him tied under his horse and sent back to his companions that way. Still he desires her. "Even now I'd defend her honor unto death," he declares. "I love her passionately."

Ettard's treatment of Pellias outrages Sir Brandiles and Sir Mador. They propose storming Ettard's castle and forcing her to beg Pellias's forgiveness, even if they have to "drag her by her hair." Pellias responds, "No. You can't treat a woman that way." The code of knighthood prohibits violence toward women, who must be treated with respect. When Gawain accidentally wounds Constance, he laments, "Oh! What have I done?" His brother Gaheris says, "You've struck a shameful blow." Guinevere is greatly displeased when she learns that Gawain struck a woman, even though he did so unintentionally. "Any sword that strikes a woman is dishonored," she states, "and any knight who strikes a woman breaks his vow of knighthood." Smarting from her criticism, Gawain breaks and discards his sword.

Women and female fairies marry when and whom they choose, often after testing a man's worthiness. Ettard marries Engamore only after he repeatedly fights as her champion. Guinevere's father, who is also her king, doesn't order or even ask her to marry Arthur. Instead he offers gentle encouragement: "It would be good if you felt inclined toward him." Nymue uses magic to bring about her marriage to Pellias, whom she loves. She makes him half fairy and wears a necklace that evokes his love. But first she tests his chivalry. Assuming the appearance of an old, ugly woman, she asks Pellias to help her cross a river. He courteously puts her on his horse and brings her across. Nyneve loves Gawain. Like Nymue, she arranges a sequence of events that tests the man she loves and results in marriage. Pretending to be old and ugly, she gets Arthur to promise that she can marry whichever of his knights she chooses.

She selects Gawain, who honors the promise and treats her with consideration and respect.

The book ends with a double affirmation of female power. In order to survive, Arthur must answer this riddle: What do women most desire? Nyneve supplies the answer: to have their way. On their wedding night, Nyneve and Gawain disagree about a course of action. "I would have it *my* way," she insists. Gawain yields: "So be it, then. You'll have your way in this and all other things." He has passed his wife's final test.

King Arthur and His Knights recounts episode after episode of men's physical courage and strength. In many ways, though, the book's female characters wield the most power.

altercation: مُشاجَرة جدال

a noisy argument مُشاحَّة
or disagreement
especially in public.

Caynaab